Shire County Guide 8

SURREY

John Drewett

Shire Publications Ltd

Published in 1996 by Shire Publications Ltd, Cromwell House, Church Street, Princes Risborough, Buckinghamshire HP27 9AA, UK.
Copyright © 1985 and 1996 by John Drewett. First published 1985. Second edition 1990. Third edition, extensively revised and expanded, 1996. Shire County Guide 8. ISBN 0 7478 0310 2.
John Drewett is hereby identified as the author of this work in accordance with Section 77 of the Copyright, Designs and Patents Act 1988.

Printed in Great Britain by CIT Printing Services, Press Buildings, Merlins Bridge, Haverfordwest, Dyfed SA61 1XF.

British Library Cataloguing in Publication Data: Drewett, John, 1958 - Surrey. - (Shire county guide; 8) 1. Surrey (England) - Guidebooks I. Title 914.2'21'04859 ISBN 0-7478-0310-2

Acknowledgements

Photographs on pages 10, 13, 26, 32, 36 (upper), 41 (lower), 45 (both), 48 (lower), 63, 67, 68 and 96 (upper) are by the author. The others, including the cover, are by Cadbury Lamb. The map on pages 4 and 5 is by Robert Dizon, using Ordnance Survey material. The National Grid References in the text are included by permission of the Controller of Her Majesty's Stationery Office.

Ordnance Survey grid references

Although information on how to reach most of the places described in this book by car is given in the text, National Grid References are also included in many instances, particularly for the harder-to-find places in chapters 3, 4 and 8, for the benefit of those readers who have the Ordnance Survey 1:50,000 Landranger maps of the area. The references are stated as a Landranger sheet number followed by the 100 km National Grid square and the six-figure reference.

To locate a site by means of the grid references, proceed as in the following example: Box Hill Country Park (OS 187: TQ 179513). Take the OS Landranger map sheet 187 (Dorking, Reigate and Crawley area). The grid numbers are printed in blue around the edges of the map. (In more recently produced maps these numbers are repeated at 10 km intervals throughout the map, so that it is not necessary to open it out completely.) Read off these numbers from the left along the top edge of the map until you come to 17, denoting a vertical grid line, then estimate nine-tenths of the distance to vertical line 18 and envisage an imaginary vertical grid line 17.9 at this point. Next look at the grid numbers at one side of the map (either side will do) and read *upwards* until you find the horizontal grid line 51. Estimate three-tenths of the distance to the next horizontal line above (i.e. 52), and so envisage an imaginary horizontal line across the map at 51.3. Follow this imaginary line across the map until it crosses the imaginary vertical line 17.9. At the intersection of these two lines you will find Box Hill Country Park.

The Ordnance Survey Landranger maps which cover Surrey are sheets 175, 176, 186 and 187. A very small area of the county is found on map 177.

Cover: *The Old Town Hall at Godalming, known as 'The Pepperpot'.*

Contents

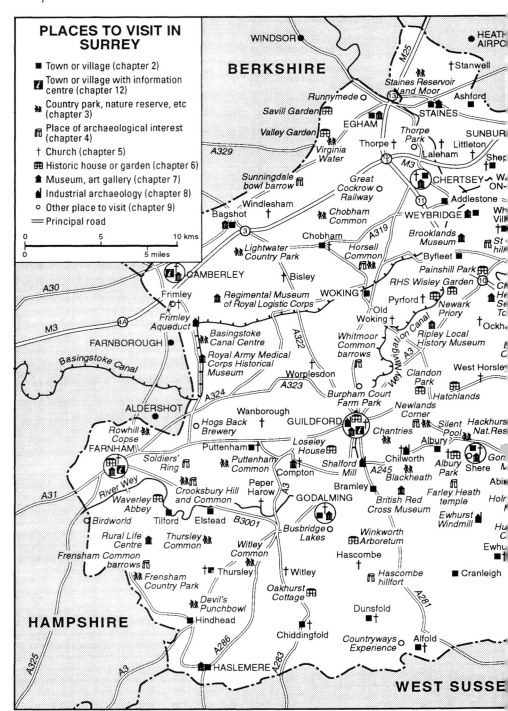

4

PLACES TO VISIT IN SURREY

- ■ Town or village (chapter 2)
- 🖳 Town or village with information centre (chapter 12)
- 🕴 Country park, nature reserve, etc (chapter 3)
- 🏛 Place of archaeological interest (chapter 4)
- † Church (chapter 5)
- ⊞ Historic house or garden (chapter 6)
- 🏛 Museum, art gallery (chapter 7)
- 🔨 Industrial archaeology (chapter 8)
- ○ Other place to visit (chapter 9)
- ══ Principal road

0   5   10 kms
0   5 miles

WINDSOR
HEATH
AIRPO

BERKSHIRE

† Stanwell

Staines Reservoir and Moor
Ashford

Runnymede ○
STAINES

Savill Garden ⊞

EGHAM
Thorpe
Park
SUNBUR

Valley Garden ⊞
Thorpe †
Littleton

A329
Virginia
Water
Laleham †
Shep
†■

Sunningdale
bowl barrow 🏛
Great
Cockrow ○
Railway
M3
CHERTSEY
W
ON-

Windlesham
Addlestone

Bagshot †
Chobham
Common
WEYBRIDGE 🏛 ■
Wh
Vill

Lightwater
Country Park
Chobham
Horsell
Common
Brooklands
Museum 🏛
St
hill

CAMBERLEY
† Bisley
WOKING ■
RHS Wisley Garden
Painshill Park ⊞

Frimley †
Regimental Museum
of Royal Logistic Corps
Pyrford †
Newark
Priory
C
He
Se
To

M3
Frimley
Aqueduct
Old
Woking †
Whitmoor
Common
barrows 🏛
Ripley Local
History Museum
† Ockh

FARNBOROUGH ●
Basingstoke
Canal Centre
Basingstoke Canal
Royal Army Medical
Corps Historical
Museum
Worplesdon
A323
Clandon
Park ⊞
West Horsle

A324
Burpham Court
Farm Park
Newlands
Corner
Hatchlands

ALDERSHOT ●
Wanborough
GUILDFORD
Silent
Pool
Hackhurs
Nat.Res

Rowhill
Copse 🕴
Hogs Back
Brewery
Chantries
Albury
FARNHAM
Puttenham ■
Loseley
House ⊞
Chilworth
Albury
Park
Shere
Gom
M

Soldiers'
Ring 🏛
Puttenham
Common
Shalford
Mill
A245
Blackheath
Abi

River Wey
Peper
Harow
Compton
Bramley ■
Farley Heath
temple
Holr

Crooksbury Hill
and Common
GODALMING
British Red
Cross Museum
Ewhurst
Windmill 🔨

Waverley
Abbey ⊞
Tilford
Elstead
B3001
Busbridge ○
Lakes
Winkworth
⊞ Arboretum
Hu
C

Birdworld ○
Rural Life
Centre 🏛
Thursley
Common
Witley
Common
Hascombe
†
Ewhu
■ †

Frensham Common
barrows 🏛
Frensham
Country Park
† ■ Thursley
† Witley
Hascombe
hillfort 🏛
■ Cranleigh

Devil's
Punchbowl
Oakhurst
Cottage ⊞

■ Hindhead
Dunsfold
■ †

A286
Chiddingfold
Countryways
Experience ○
Alfold
■ †

HAMPSHIRE
HASLEMERE
WEST SUSSE

Preface

Welcome to the Shire County Guide to Surrey, one of over thirty such books, written and designed to enable you to organise your time in the county well.

The Shire County Guides fill the need for a compact, accurate and thorough guide to each county so that visitors can plan a half-day excursion or a whole week's stay to best advantage. Residents, too, will find the guides a handy and reliable reference to the places of interest in their area.

Travelling British roads can be time consuming, and the County Guides will ensure that you need not inadvertently miss any interesting feature in a locality, that you do not accidentally bypass a new museum or an outstanding church, that you can find an attractive place to picnic, and that you will appreciate the history and the buildings of the towns or villages in which you stop.

This book has been arranged in special interest chapters, such as the countryside, historic buildings and gardens or places of archaeological interest, and all these places are located on the map on pages 4-5. Use the map either for an overview to decide which area has most to interest you, or to help you enjoy your immediate neighbourhood. Then refer to the nearest town or village in chapter 2 to see, at a glance, what special features or attractions each community contains or is near. The subsequent chapters enable readers with a particular interest to find immediately those places of importance to them, while the cross-referencing under 'Surrey Towns and Villages' assists readers with wider tastes to select how best to spend their time.

Catteshall Lock, near Godalming.

1
A surprising county

To the outsider, Surrey must be one of the most surprising of English counties. In terms of size it comes thirty-fourth, but in terms of population fourteenth. This might suggest a vastly overcrowded county in which anything of natural or historical interest has long been lost. Yet, away from the northern part, Surrey still has one of the highest proportions of open countryside anywhere in Britain.

There is little relationship between natural features and the county boundary. In the west the river Blackwater forms part of the boundary with Hampshire, whilst in the north the Thames used to be the natural boundary. However, over the centuries the northern half was gradually swallowed up by London. The London Boroughs of Richmond, Kingston, Sutton, Merton and Croydon, which comprise this northern part, still refer to themselves as Surrey, and so are included in this book. Kingston upon Thames still houses the offices of Surrey County Council, although it is no longer in the county.

In the north-east the boundary follows a Roman road for some distance, before meandering aimlessly between villages. The meandering continues along the border with Sussex too. One last change, in 1974, saw the transfer to Surrey of the remnants of Middlesex, around Staines and Ashford. This took the county boundary, for the first time, across the Thames.

Unlike political geography, the physical geography of Surrey is far more organised. The various rock formations run in bands, east to west, and the further they are from London the older they are. In Sussex, the reverse pattern can be observed, showing that south-east England was once one great dome of folded rocks, the top of which has been eroded away to leave the underlying strata exposed like the bands of a liquorice allsort.

The oldest rocks to reach the surface are the Tunbridge Wells Sands, which are found in a small area of south-east Surrey. They were deposited around 125 million years ago by large rivers running into a massive delta which covered most of Kent, East Sussex and south-east Surrey.

Weald Clay forms a broad band across the south of the county. This is the area of densest tree cover and heavy soils. Fields have been cut directly from the woods and wide sections of the original woodland have been left between fields to form dense hedges, rich in wildlife. Surrey has more trees per acre than any other county in England.

North of the Weald Clay is a substantial range of hills formed from Lower Greensand. These rocks broaden out in the west, around Hindhead, where their acidity gives rise to extensive heathlands. Further east, between Guildford and Dorking, they are more wooded. Here they are capped with chert, a hard layer which has prevented erosion. Leith Hill, at 967 feet (294 metres), is the highest point in south-east England.

Between the Greensand ridge and the North Downs two very narrow geological formations occur, Gault Clay and Upper Greensand. There are two types of Upper Greensand, known as malmstone and hearthstone. The former was once quarried in the Reigate area for building stone and the lining of furnaces. The latter, a soft greenish-grey calcareous sandstone, was once used to whiten hearths.

The prime rock of the North Downs is chalk. The south scarp of the Downs drops steeply towards the Weald, whilst the north face slopes more gently into the London Basin. Between Guildford and Farnham the chalk ridge narrows, with steep slopes on both sides, and is known as the Hog's Back.

The North Downs ridge is broken only twice in Surrey: at Guildford by the river Wey, and between Dorking and Leatherhead by the river Mole. Where the Mole flows around the foot of Box Hill a spectacular river cliff has developed, following thousands of years of erosion. This cliff is clothed with box and yew trees and the hill is named after the former species.

In some places the northern slopes of the

Downs are broken by steep parallel dry valleys. This is particularly a feature of the Box Hill district. These valleys were carved from the chalk by meltwater during the ice ages, when underground seepage could not occur because of the frozen ground. Unlike today, surplus water flowed over the surface in streams and rivers. The Downs, where not covered by trees, are important places for orchids and other wild flowers, together with their associated insect fauna.

The two most recent geological formations in the county, London Clay and Bagshot Beds, occur in the north. London Clay covers most of north-east Surrey and the south London boroughs. Much of it is now built upon, but where open country still exists grassy commons or oak woodlands may be found. Examples can be seen at Ashtead, Epsom and Bookham commons.

The wild open heathlands of north-west Surrey lie mainly on the Bagshot Beds. These consist of fine buff-coloured sands and flint pebbles. Large parts of this heathland are open to the public but some are used for military training. In both cases wildlife flourishes, as at Chobham Common, recently declared a National Nature Reserve.

Surrey heathland is of tremendous importance. Not only does it support a wide variety of insects and animals, either rare or on the edge of their range, but it occurs in large enough blocks to make these populations viable. Thursley Common, another National Nature Reserve, is one of the most important sites for dragonflies in north-west Europe.

The average farm in Surrey is smaller than in other parts of Britain, yet 40 per cent of the county is devoted to agriculture and horticulture. The extensive areas of clay to the north and south of the Downs are not very suitable for cereal crops, but some areas of wheat and barley do exist. Much farmland in these places has been put down to grass, used for grazing dairy and beef cattle. Sheep have become an important component of Surrey farming. Even the National Trust slopes of the North Downs are now grazed by sheep in an attempt to maintain the open grasslands, rich in wild flowers. In addition, Surrey has areas of most other crops, including fruits, which have of-

ten been planted as 'pick-your-own' farms. There is even a small but increasing area of vines, producing well-respected English wine.

A high proportion of Surrey woodland remains broad-leaved. As a result, there are fine displays of spring flowers such as bluebell and wood anemone. However, where woods were coppiced in the past for making hurdles or broom handles, dense regrowth is shading out some of these plants owing to lack of management.

Water plays a surprisingly important part in this landlocked county. Apart from the rivers Mole and Wey, the Thames flows through the north of Surrey. Much of north-west Surrey lies on Thames gravels which have been much exploited for construction materials. Gravel extraction has led to the creation of lakes in many old gravel pits, thus supplementing the existing bodies of water. Also in this area, large reservoirs have been constructed to supply London. and have become important sites for wintering birds.

Today, Surrey is well and truly commuter land. A dense web of roads and railways extend long fingers from the capital. Along their length have grown towns and villages, many of the inhabitants of which work in London. To the north of the Downs these have more or less joined to form a continuous suburbia, but beyond its fringes strict Green Belt policies have retained a good deal of rural landscape, since their introduction in the 1930s.

Since 1931, when the Surrey County Council Act first permitted the acquisition of large tracts of countryside for purposes other than building, this authority has become the custodian of extensive areas of the county.

Another major landowner in Surrey is the National Trust. It protects several thousand acres of countryside, ranging from woodland and heathland to orchid-rich chalk grassland.

Private estates, too, manage extensive stretches of countryside, most of which are accessible by means of a well-used network of public rights of way. Along with smaller organisations like the Surrey Wildlife Trust, they have done much to maintain the beauty and diversity that makes Surrey one of England's most diverse counties, despite being one of the smallest.

2
Surrey towns and villages

Abinger

The parish of Abinger stretches for 9½ miles (15 km) north to south. Frequent changes in the underlying geological formations, which run east to west, made long narrow parishes the most practical way of ensuring each had its share of rich and poor soils.

Three settlements include the word Abinger in their names. The largest, **Abinger Hammer**, straddles the A25. It derives its name from the hammers of the ironworking mills which prospered here in medieval times. Today the hammer ponds, which provided the water to power the mills, are planted with watercress. A clock which projects over the road is a reminder of the ironworking days. Dating from 1903, the bell is struck by 'Jack the Smith' every hour.

A short distance to the south is **Sutton Abinger**. Although surrounded to some extent by more recent buildings, the core of this settlement is a small group of timber-framed cottages along a single-track lane.

Further to the south-east lies the scattered settlement of **Abinger Common**. It has been claimed that this is the English village with the longest period of occupation, having a mesolithic pit dwelling and a superb Norman castle motte, excavated in 1949. However, there is no evidence to suggest that occupation has been continuous. The earth mound of the castle stands in the grounds of the Manor House, behind the church. It can be viewed from the public footpath alongside. When in use, a wooden palisade would have been erected on top of the mound, with a wooden tower inside it. The castle was never rebuilt in stone.

In front of St James's church, the village stocks may be seen, preserved behind iron railings. At the south end of Abinger Common stands a well, erected in 1893. Nearby is a house called Goddards, designed by Lutyens.

Between Abinger Common and Abinger Hammer, Abinger Mill may be seen from the road. Once a corn mill and now a private house, this picturesque old cottage has been the site of several other mills, which in their times produced gunpowder and copper plate.

A medieval fair is held in the village each June (page 115).

Abinger pit dwelling, page 62; **church of St James**, page 66.

In the locality: Deerleap Wood bell barrow, page 63; Ewhurst Windmill, page 103; Farley Heath Romano-British temple, page 63; Gomshall Mill, page 104; Hackhurst Local Nature Reserve, page 53; Holmbury hillfort, page 64; Hurtwood Control, page 53; Leith Hill, page 54; the Old Farm at Shere, page 109; Shere Museum, page 100; and churches at Ewhurst, page 70; Shere, page 73; and Wotton, page 75.

Addington

Church of St Mary, page 66.

Addlestone

A commuter district for London, Addlestone is largely a mixture of nineteenth- and twentieth-century architecture. Scattered throughout the area are the occasional older buildings such as the sixteenth-century Sayes Court Lodge in Liberty Lane.

In the locality: Brooklands Museum, page 100; Chertsey Museum, page 92; Elmbridge Museum, page 101; Great Cockrow Railway, page 108; St George's hillfort, page 64; Thorpe Park, page 109; the Wey Navigation Canal, page 60; and churches at Chertsey, page 68; and Thorpe, page 75.

Albury

The visitor to this small village, tucked into a fold in the hills below Newlands Corner, will most likely recall the numerous elaborate chimneys dominating the skyline above the main street of attractive cottages. Albury is

Cottages by the church in Alfold.

on the tiny river Tillingbourne, which slips past at the back of the houses.

The original village was clustered around the mansion in Albury Park. In the nineteenth century the owner had it demolished and replaced by the present estate village, at what was then Weston Street. The past has left Albury with three churches; one is semi-ruined in the park; another is the current parish church, whilst the third is the closed Catholic Apostolic church, looking like a small cathedral from the Silent Pool.

Albury Park, page 76; **church of St Peter and St Paul**, page 66; **Silent Pool**, page 58.

In the locality: Blackheath, page 50; Chilworth Gunpowder Mills, page 103; Hackhurst Local Nature Reserve, page 53; Newlands Corner, page 55; Newlands Corner round barrow, page 64; The Old Farm at Shere, page 109; Shere Museum, page 100; and churches at Chilworth, page 68; and Shere, page 73.

Alfold

The most attractive aspect of Alfold is the approach to St Nicholas's church, which is bordered by two picturesque cottages. Much of the remainder is made up of a string of hamlets. By the main road, half a mile (800 metres) north-east of the church, stands Alfold House. This timber-framed house is probably sixteenth-century and exhibits a wide range of timberwork. The roof is typical of old houses in this area, being of heavy Horsham stone.

Excavations in the woodland surrounding the village have produced evidence of the medieval glass industry, for which the district is famed.

Church of St Nicholas, page 66; **Countryways Experience**, page 108.

In the locality: churches at Chiddingfold, page 68; and Dunsfold, page 69.

Ashford

Little remains of the old village of Ashford. Today the area is almost entirely suburban, and the centre is a selection of modern shops. Spelthorne College, in the town centre, is, however, an elegant symmetrical building. Ashford is close to several reservoirs where there are facilities for sailing, fishing and birdwatching.

In the locality: Spelthorne Museum, page 100; Staines Reservoir and Moor, page 58; and churches at Laleham, page 71; Littleton, page 71; Shepperton, page 73; and Stanwell, page 74.

Ashtead

The overgrown village of Ashtead fills most of the space between Epsom and Leatherhead. Ashtead Common, on the London Clay, is an excellent area for walks, although very wet in winter. Part of the common has ancient oak woodland, where the trees are massive. The common was an important site for tilemaking during the Roman period. The site where the tile works and Roman villa were excavated can still be made out when the bracken is low. The clay pits are clearly visible nearby.

On the other side of the village is Ashtead Park, an open space owned by the local authority. The meadows, woodland and lakes here are a haven for wildlife. Also in the park are the church of St Giles and Ashtead Park House, now the City of London Freemen's School. It is the only complete neo-classical house in Surrey.

Church of St Giles, page 66.

In the locality: Chessington World of Adventures, page 107; Epsom Common, page 52; Leatherhead Museum of Local History, page 98; Nower Wood, page 56; and church at Leatherhead, page 71.

Ash Vale

Royal Army Medical Corps Historical Museum, page 91.

Bagshot

Bagshot is a small town with buildings around a square, dominated by a large railway viaduct. Once this area was barren heathland frequented by highwaymen. Today it is a centre for the army.

In the early nineteenth century Bagshot Park, across the A30 from the town, was the home of the Duchess of Gloucester. Her garden foreman, John Standish, soon established his own nursery business growing fuchsias and calceolarias. He developed a contact with Robert Fortune, who was at that time introducing many exotic plants to Britain, and was soon propagating these too. He became a devotee of rhododendrons and was one of the forerunners of the large nurseries now to be found in this part of Surrey.

Museum of the Royal Army Chaplains Department, page 91.

In the locality: Chobham Common, page 51; Lightwater Country Park, page 54; Regimental Museum of the Royal Logistic Corps, page 91; Staff College Museum, page 91; Surrey Heath Museum, page 91; Virginia Water, page 59; and church at Windlesham, page 75.

Banstead

Despite being signposted 'Banstead Village', Banstead is a small town. It has its own modern shopping street, where most everyday goods can be purchased. Being close to Epsom, there is easy access to Epsom Downs and the racecourse. Oaks Park House gave its name to the famous Oaks race meeting.

In Park Road, in a white-painted, roofed structure in the centre of the road, is the village well. The covered building was erected in the eighteenth century. Beyond the well are Rosehill (1730) and the weatherboarded Woodmans Cottages. A Norman Shaw house in the wildlife-rich Banstead Wood now serves as a hospital.

Banstead Woods, Fames Rough and Park Downs, page 49.

In the locality: Bourne Hall Museum, page 95; Epsom Common, page 52; Whitehall, page 87; and church at Lower Kingswood page 71.

Beddington

Carew Manor and Dovecote, page 76; church of St Mary, page 66.

Betchworth

A small village nucleus is centred on St Michael's church, with other interesting buildings scattered over a wider area. Next to the churchyard, in a short cul-de-sac, is an old barn, built in the seventeenth century. Opposite the Old Vicarage are three sixteenth-century timber-framed cottages, followed by three of eighteenth-century construction. Near the bottom of Church Street is The Gardens, a sixteenth-century smoke-bay house. The stark-looking eighteenth-century façade of Old House hides a much older building behind. Other old buildings in The Street include the Dolphin Inn, The Forge, Old Mill Cottage and Dillon Cottage. The last two are the oldest in Betchworth.

There are several large houses around the village, among which Betchworth House, built in 1634, was the manor house. It is largely hidden by a high wall, alongside which runs a raised footpath for use in the event of flood. The river Mole, the cause of these floods, rises near Gatwick Airport, passing the once important watermill at Wonham on its way to the Thames. Before Wonham Mill is reached, More Place is passed. This is a most attractive fifteenth-century house, much altered, with grounds sloping down to the river.

Betchworth is set amid attractive countryside with the opportunity for many walks, including one to nearby Brockham.

Betchworth Chalk Quarries, page 102; **church of St Michael**, page 66.

In the locality: Box Hill Country Park, page 51; Reigate Heath barrows, page 64; Reigate Heath windmill, page 105.

Bisley

Church of St John the Baptist, page 66.

Blechingley

Although the Ordnance Survey spells it 'Bletchingley', any local will tell you it is 'Blechingley'. In the early thirteenth century it was a borough and thriving market town, where the fulling and weaving industries were developing. Today it is a large street village, arranged around the old market place, where the High Street broadens in the east.

The buildings include a wide range of cottages, many tile-hung. Those in the west are mostly eighteenth-century or later, whilst those in the east, around St Mary's church and the market place, are all of earlier date. A very attractive group can be seen in Church Walk, which leads to the large, partly Norman church. South of the A25, off Castle Square, there was once a castle, but it was short-lived and nothing remains today. It was

situated on the edge of the steep ridge at the top of the street, from where there are excellent views over the Weald. To the north of the village are Brewer Street Farmhouse, a fifteenth-century timber-framed hall-house, and the sixteenth-century brick Pendell Court. **Church of St Mary**, page 67; **South Park Farm**, page 58.

In the locality: Fire Brigades of Surrey Preservation Trust, page 99; Godstone Farm, page 108; Outwood Common Windmill, page 105; Surrey Iron Railway, page 105; and churches at Merstham, page 71; and Outwood, page 72.

Bramley

Bramley is a long street village on the Guildford to Horsham road, in the valley formed by Cranleigh Water. There was once a canal here, linking the rivers Wey and Arun to form a route from London to the sea. This has long been abandoned as a commercial venture but is being restored. Traces of the railway which linked Guildford to Shoreham-by-Sea in West Sussex can also be seen. This now forms part of a long-distance walk, the Downs Link. Chinthurst Hill, to the north-east, also provides pleasant walks.

The village has many listed buildings dating from the fifteenth to nineteenth centuries. Among these are Bramley Mill and Snowdenham Mill, both of which were working into the twentieth century. Timber-framed East Manor House is mid sixteenth-century, whilst Millmead is by Sir Edwin Lutyens, built in 1904-7.

Downs Link, page 52.

In the locality: Blackheath, page 50; British Red Cross Museum and Archives, page 101; Chilworth Gunpowder Mills, page 103; Godalming Museum, page 95; Hascombe hillfort, page 63; Shalford Mill, page 105; Winkworth Arboretum, page 90; and churches at Chilworth, page 68; Godalming, page 70; and Hascombe, page 71.

Brockham

The perfect picture-postcard village, Brockham has a large neat village green, surrounded by cottages, with a church at one end. To the north rise the slopes of Box Hill,

Brewer Street Farmhouse in Blechingley.

complementing the perfect smoothness of the green.

Flowing past Brockham is the river Mole, along the banks of which a footpath leads to Betchworth. South of the village, at Strood Green, is an area of Forestry Commission woodland with a range of attractive walks. The North Downs Way crosses the slopes of Box Hill before passing through the disused chalk quarries above the village.

In the locality: Betchworth Chalk Quarries, page 102; Box Hill Country Park, page 51; Denbies Wine Estate, page 108; Dorking and District Museum, page 94; and churches at Betchworth, page 66; and Dorking, page 69.

Burstow
Church of St Bartholomew, page 67.

Byfleet
Until the 1940s Byfleet was a scattered village near the river Wey. Since then there has been a building boom, and the village has become an attractive area of suburbia. The church, once isolated, is now surrounded by housing but retains its rural dignity. In the churchyard is a very unusual graveboard, close to the lychgate.

Some of the big houses of old Byfleet remain. In High Road are three eighteenth-century buildings of interest: the Clock House, Manor Cottage and Oak Tree Cottage. Close by, in Mill Lane, the Manor House dates from 1686, whilst Byfleet Mill House and the Water Mill are eighteenth century. The Manor House is particularly fine, situated in a secluded position by the riverside.

The river Wey is alive with small water creatures and is much used for canoeing. Wild hops grow in profusion in many parts of Byfleet.

Wey Navigation Canal, page 60.

In the locality: Brooklands Museum, page 100; Chatley Heath Semaphore Tower, page 92; Cobham Bus Museum, page 93; Cobham Mill, page 103; Elmbridge Museum, page 101; Newark Priory, page 82; Painshill Park, page 83; Royal Horticultural Society's Wisley Garden, page 85; and churches at Cobham, page 69; Ockham, page 72; and Pyrford, page 73.

Camberley
This sprawling town grew up after the Royal Military College moved to Sandhurst in 1809. The original part, York Town, is based around a grid of streets and named after the Duke of York. The town centre is largely a mixture of Victorian and modern architecture interspersed with numerous flowerbeds and occasional fountains. The town is surrounded

Surrey Heath District Council offices in Camberley.

by attractive heathland with many interesting species of wildlife. The Civic Hall in Knoll Road provides a wide range of entertainment throughout the year, from art exhibitions to variety shows.

Church of St Paul, page 67; **Regimental Museum of the Royal Logistic Corps**, page 91; **Staff College Museum**, page 91; **Surrey Heath Museum**, page 91.

In the locality: Basingstoke Canal Centre, page 49; Blackwater Valley Visitor Centre, page 107; Frimley Aqueduct, page 103; Museum of the Royal Army Chaplains Department, page 91; Royal Army Medical Corps Historical Museum, page 91; and church at Frimley, page 70.

Capel

Set in the Weald, Capel is a quiet village now that it has been bypassed. There are extensive tracts of countryside in the area, including two nature reserves of the Surrey Wildlife Trust. A bridleway passes through one of these, alongside the beautiful Vann Lake, set in a steep wooded valley.

South of the main part of the village, on the border with West Sussex, stands a group of large old farmhouses in which timber-framing is a major element of the construction. Among

the best of these are Osbrooks Farm and Bonnetts Farm. Many old barns also remain, providing homes for the now uncommon barn owl.

In the locality: Gatwick Zoo, page 108; Lowfield Heath Windmill, page 104; Vann Lake, page 59; and church at Newdigate, page 72.

Carshalton

Situated between Sutton and Croydon, this south London village is unique. At its centre are two ponds, crossed by a pretty bridge, and around which are arranged many old buildings. Away from the surrounding suburbia, there is a core of old houses, a park and the source of the river Wandle. At Carshalton House there is an impressive early eighteenth-century water tower attributed to Henry Joynes. In Festival Walk is Owls, the Sutton Ecology Centre.

Carshalton Heritage Centre, page 91; **church of All Saints**, page 67; **Little Holland House**, page 82.

In the locality: Banstead Woods, page 49; Carew Manor and Dovecote, page 76; Croydon Clocktower, page 94; Croydon Old Palace, page 78; Morden Hall Park, page 55; Whitehall, page 87; and church at Beddington, page 66.

Caterham

Caterham developed from a downland village after the arrival of the railway in 1856. The town first grew up in the valley around the station. Later, in the 1930s, housing spread southwards to engulf the old village itself. Remnants of the village buildings can be seen in the main street of Caterham-on-the-Hill. At the end of this street, the old church of St Lawrence stands opposite the much larger nineteenth-century church. East Surrey Museum is situated near the station. South-west of the town, on the corner of War Coppice Road, can be found the remains of a derelict folly tower of about 1800. Further along this road, on the south side, are the uncompleted embankments of an iron age hillfort.

Church of St Lawrence, page 67; **East Surrey Museum**, page 91.

In the locality: Godstone Farm, page 108; Surrey Iron Railway, page 105; and churches at Chaldon, page 67; Chelsham, page 68; Coulsdon, page 69; Farleigh, page 70; and Merstham, page 71.

Chaldon

Church of St Peter and St Paul, page 67.

Charlwood

Church of St Nicholas, page 68; Gatwick Zoo, page 108; Lowfield Heath Windmill, page 104; Providence Chapel, page 68.

Cheam

Whitehall, page 87.

Chelsham

Church of St Leonard, page 68.

Chertsey

Market day Saturday.

Chertsey lies alongside the Thames, on the gravels formed in the Thames and Wey valleys. Across the river, the large areas of flooded gravel pits testify to this underlying geology. The area occupied by the town was once a marshy island surrounded by rivers until Benedictine monks confined the waters. Chertsey Abbey was founded in 666 and destroyed by the Danes in the ninth century. It was subsequently refounded in the eleventh century. Following the Dissolution in 1537, stone was robbed for other buildings, leaving no trace today.

In the early eighteenth century it became

Chertsey Old Town Hall in London Street.

fashionable to move out of London, leading to a marked increase in building in Chertsey, but it was not until the arrival of the railway in 1848 that expansion accelerated. Until then the economy was based on agriculture, market gardening and brickmaking. Despite modern redevelopment, the three main streets of Chertsey retain a considerable amount of their eighteenth-century architecture. Mostly these are Grade II listed buildings.

In London Street stands the 1851 Old Town Hall, an Italianate building, the lower floor of which covers the pavement with an open five-arched colonnade. To the east of the town centre is Chertsey Bridge, built between 1780 and 1785 by a local man, James Paine. This twelve-arch bridge was altered in 1894. There are walks along the Thames towpath, beginning near the town, and good views from St Anne's Hill, an old hill camp and ancient monument. Finds illustrating the past history and archaeology of Chertsey are housed in the museum.

Chertsey Museum, page 92; **church of St Peter**, page 68; **Thorpe Park**, page 109.

In the locality:- Brooklands Museum, page 100; Chobham Common, page 51; Egham Museum, page 95; Elmbridge Museum, page 101; Great Cockrow Railway, page 108; Picture Gallery, Royal Holloway College, page 95; and churches at Laleham, page 71; Shepperton, page 73; and Thorpe, page 75.

Chessington

Chessington World of Adventures, page 107.

Chiddingfold

Near the Sussex border, Chiddingfold is a large pretty village mostly gathered around an enormous triangular green. First recorded in the twelfth century, it has many of the components which make up the perfect English village: a group of old cottages, an inn, church and pond. The inn is probably more than five hundred years old. It is a massive timber-framed building with a good crown-post roof.

During the thirteenth century Chiddingfold became an important centre of the Wealden glass industry. This is commemorated by a plaque in the church, below a window made of old glass fragments. Until the industry ceased in the seventeenth century, the village supplied stained glass for many buildings, including St Stephen's, Westminster.

Many of the cottages in Chiddingfold are irregular and tile-hung. To the east is the Old Manor House, an elegant eighteenth-century five-bay house with a Tuscan Doric doorcase. Nearby, in a side lane, the old village pound stands in the garden of Pound Cottage.

At Pickhurst, to the south-east, is a large tile-hung house of 1883, near to some woodland where medieval glass furnaces have been found. Roman buildings were excavated at High Ridings near Chiddingfold in the year Pickhurst was built and date from the early second to mid third century AD. Nothing is now visible on the surface.

Church of St Mary the Virgin, page 68.

In the locality: Educational Museum, page 97; Oakhurst Cottage, page 83; and church at Dunsfold, page 69.

Chilworth

Chilworth Gunpowder Mills, page 103; church of St Martha on the Hill, page 68.

Chobham

This is a neat street village between Chobham Common and Horsell Common. With its large collection of old buildings, Chobham is situated on alluvial gravels, deposited by the many small streams in the area.

Chobham Common, page 51; **church of St Laurence**, page 69.

In the locality: Lightwater Country Park, page 54; and churches at Bisley, page 66; and Windlesham, page 75.

Cobham

Cobham is a small town set beside an attractive stretch of the river Mole. The most interesting buildings are around St Andrew's church and along Church Street. Despite the date on the front (1432), Church Stile House is of early seventeenth-century construction. Its two upper floors are jettied, in the style of many timber-framed houses. Nearby Lime House, a well-proportioned brick building, was built about 1740. At the top of Church

The view across Chiddingfold pond to the church.

Street, a restaurant occupies a fifteenth-century hall-house. Churchgate House, across the churchyard, is tile-hung. It adjoins pretty ogee-windowed Rose Lodge. Other interesting buildings include Cedar House, near the river, and the Vermont Exchange, at the west end of the town. Both are of brick, the former being fronted by fine iron gates.

A short distance to the south is Downside, where attractive cottages surround a large open green. On one side is a minute chapel, with a pump in front. A mile or so to the west, in Redhill Road, the Model Farm of Foxwarren Park may be seen. The many gabled buildings are an extreme example of Victorian eccentricity. Nearby is the Cobham Bus Museum.

Church of St Andrew, page 69; **Chatley Heath Semaphore Tower**, page 92; **Cobham Bus Museum**, page 93; **Cobham Mill**, page 103; **Painshill Park**, page 83.

In the locality: Bocketts Farm Park, page 107; Bookham Commons, page 50; Brooklands Museum, page 100; Claremont House, page 76; Claremont Landscape Garden, page 77; Elmbridge Museum, page 101; Royal Horticul- *tural Society's Wisley Garden, page 85; and churches at Esher, page 70; Fetcham, page 70; Ockham, page 72; Stoke D'Abernon, page 74; and Whiteley Village, page 75.*

Coldharbour
Anstiebury hillfort, page 62.

Compton
Church of St Nicholas, page 69; Watts Gallery, page 93.

Coulsdon
Old Coulsdon was part of the lands of Chertsey Abbey for eight hundred years. In 1537, the manor was purchased from Henry VIII by Sir Nicholas Carew. Unfortunately for him, he was executed for high treason two years later.

A large part of Coulsdon is suburban development, strung out along the A23. Away from this, however, there are some delightful corners, especially around the church of St John the Evangelist. This is beautifully positioned beside a large green, the rural impression being intensified by a nearby sixteenth-century barn.

Close by, at Farthing Downs, a group of well-preserved lynchets – banks marking the boundaries of ancient fields – may be seen. A Saxon burial ground has also been excavated in the vicinity.

Church of St John the Evangelist, page 69.

In the locality: Croydon Clocktower, page 94; Croydon Old Palace, page 78; East Surrey Museum, page 91; Surrey Iron Railway, page 105; and churches at Caterham, page 67; Chaldon, page 67; and Merstham, page 71.

Cranleigh

It is somewhat ironic that this town, which still calls itself a village, expanded rapidly following the closure of its railway. This has left Cranleigh a pleasant residential town, but rather isolated amid wooded countryside.

At one end is a large triangular green, surrounded by cottages. The main street is lined by trees, with architecture mostly of the nineteenth and twentieth centuries. Stockland Square, a neat shopping square, occupies the site of the old railway station. Nearly op-

posite are a fountain and war memorial sporting the emblem of Cranleigh – a crane.

In 1794 a turnpike was opened from Guildford to Horsham, via Cranleigh. An obelisk built at this time to commemorate the event can be seen near the arts centre. Also in the vicinity, Cranleigh Cottage Hospital is claimed to have been the first village hospital in England, opened in 1859.

In the locality: Countryways Experience, page 108; Ewhurst Windmill, page 103; Hurtwood Control, page 53; and churches at Alfold, page 66; Dunsfold, page 69; Ewhurst, page 70; and Oakwoodhill, page 72.

Crowhurst

A range of dwellings, extending over a long distance, make up Crowhurst parish. The village is more a group of houses scattered along a road near St George's church. It is totally remote and unspoilt, having been bypassed by the railways.

Crowhurst Place, the local manor house, is approached through a mock-Tudor gatehouse, built around 1920 by George Crawley. The house itself is an early fifteenth-century hall-house, built for the Gaynesford family around 1425. The building was extensively altered and extended by Crawley in an exceptionally sympathetic manner in 1920.

The first mention of Crowhurst was in 1189, but the formation of a separate parish did not come about until the thirteenth century. The area has always been largely agricultural, although the remains of a brickworks may still be seen. The best examples of this agricultural heritage are late sixteenth-century Hobbs Farm and, opposite the church, seventeenth-century Mansion House Farm.

Church of St George, page 69.

In the locality: Haxted Mill, page 98; Staffhurst Wood, page 58; and church at Lingfield, page 71.

Croydon

Market days Monday to Saturday.

Croydon is located near the junction of several dry valleys where the Roman road from London to Portslade passes through a gap in

The covered fountain surmounted by a crane in Cranleigh.

the North Downs. In the Wandle valley Croydon, Mitcham and Beddington have yielded important finds from a series of Saxon cemeteries. Key-shaped objects called girdle hangers have been found during excavations. Although purely symbolic, they recall the female association with the Saxon house and are otherwise rare in south-east England.

In the ninth century Viking raiders landed in East Anglia and spent the winter of 871-2 in London. They probably used the city as a base for raiding Kent. An associated Viking hoard was recovered during excavations in Croydon in 1862. Two centuries later, at the time of Domesday and for long afterwards, the Lords of the Manor were the Archbishops of Canterbury. Indeed, the town's most interesting building remains their Old Palace.

Improvements to the key road to the south coast encouraged the development of Croydon. Communication was particularly important to the many waterside industries in the Wandle valley. In Cobbett's time the Wandle valley was considered one of the most industrialised parts of England, on a parallel with the textile areas of Yorkshire and Lancashire. James Malcolm's *Compendium* recorded the presence of sixteen calico and printing works, nine flour mills, five snuff mills, four oilseed-crushing mills, a paper mill, a sawmill, a copper refinery, an ironworks and a brewery in just 9 miles (14 km) of river in 1805. By the nineteenth century a tramway, a canal and a railway were providing additional links to the capital.

Its proximity and easy access to London, along with extensive wartime bombing, have ensured that Croydon has developed into a large modern town. In 1915 an aerodrome opened nearby to defend London and by 1920 had become London's first airport.

Despite its present appearance, Croydon is a town with a long history. The bustling Surrey Street market, originally the 'Fleshemarkett', has been established for more than seven hundred years. There is an excellent shopping centre, including one of the largest department stores in Britain. Fairfield Halls provide entertainment and shows of West End standard and space for art exhibitions.

Church of St John the Baptist, page 69; **Croydon Clocktower**, page 94; **Croydon Old Palace**, page 78; **Croydon Open Spaces**, page 51.

In the locality: Carew Manor and Dovecote, page 76; Carshalton Heritage Centre, page 91; Deen City Farm, page 108; Little Holland House, page 82; Wandle Industrial Museum, page 99; churches at Addington, page 66; Beddington, page 66; Carshalton, page 67; Chelsham, page 68; Coulsdon, page 69; and Farleigh, page 70.

Dorking
Market day Friday.

Dorking is an attractive market town set amid wooded hills and dominated by the spire of its parish church, St Martin's. It is situated at one of the busiest crossroads in the south-east, where the A24 meets the A25. Although Dorking stands on the Roman Stane Street and Roman remains have been found during excavations in the town, no conclusive proof of settlement has been forthcoming. It is also close to the Pilgrim's Way to Canterbury.

In the centre, where the High Street broadens into the one-time market place, is the rambling White Horse Hotel. Although the front of this old coaching inn dates largely from the eighteenth and nineteenth centuries, there are earlier, timber-framed sections behind. At the western end of the High Street is a small group of specialist shops around a courtyard, in what was once the seventeenth-century King's Head, which is said to have been the model for Dickens's Marquis of Granby in *Pickwick Papers*. Nearby a small shop with leaded windows was another inn, the Wheatsheaf.

Although the trade has declined in recent years, West Street is still a major centre of the antiques trade, with buyers coming from all over Europe. Just off the street is Dorking Museum, housed in the old Dorking Foundry. Visitors wishing to visit the sandstone caves in South Street should apply to the museum.

There are two irregular-shaped open spaces in the town, surrounded by cottages. One, Cotmandene, north of the High Street, is the site of the annual fair. The iron poles on the grass in front of the almshouses are for local people to exercise their right to air their washing. The other, Rose Hill, is approached through a mock-Tudor arch. It is a hilly green surrounded by a selection of large houses, all of differing styles.

At the eastern end of the town, opposite the Dorking Halls complex, are the modern red-brick council offices, one of the most exciting pieces of modern architecture in Surrey. In the park behind is Pippbrook, a Gothic-style building by Sir George Gilbert Scott and previously the old council offices. Just beyond the roundabout, on the road to Reigate, a footpath leads past the nineteenth-century Castle Mill, now converted into a private house, on the banks of the river Mole.

Church of St Martin, page 69; **Denbies Wine Estate**, page 108; **Dorking and District Museum**, page 94.

In the locality: Betchworth Chalk Quarries, page 102; Box Hill Country Park, page 51; Chapel Farm and Animal Trail, page 107; Deerleap Wood bell barrow, page 63; Gomshall Mill, page 104; Leith Hill, page 54; Norbury Park, page 55; Polesden Lacey, page 83; Ranmore Common, page 57; St Michael's Chapel, Westhumble, page 75; Westhumble Chapel, page 87; and churches at Betchworth, page 66; Mickleham, page 72; Newdigate, page 72; Ranmore, page 73; and Wotton, page 75.

Dormansland
Greathed Manor, page 79.

Dunsfold
Dunsfold is an attractive village in the south of the county, mostly built along one side of a large common. Unlike most Surrey villages, which are very tidy, the wild common gives Dunsfold an air of remoteness. Despite this, there are twentieth-century developments in the area, notably a well-screened airfield for testing jets. Most of the houses are brick and tile-hung, with a fair number of fifteenth-century timber-framed farms. The church is well worth a visit.

Church of St Mary and All Saints, page 69.

In the locality: Countryways Experience, page 108; and churches at Alfold, page 66;

Chiddingfold, page 68; and Hascombe, page 71.

East Clandon
Hatchlands, page 80.

East Molesey
The river Mole, which rises near Gatwick Airport in West Sussex, reaches the end of its 42 mile (67 km) journey to the Thames at East Molesey. One of the most interesting buildings in East Molesey is Hampton Court station, built in 1848-9. Situated in Bridge Street, it is Jacobean in style, in order that it may blend better with Hampton Court Palace. The bridge between Hampton Court and East Molesey is by Lutyens, the architect of many Surrey cottages, particularly around Godalming. He also designed a bridge over the Ember river, a tributary of the Mole, just under a quarter of a mile (400 metres) away.

Bell Road has several old buildings, as well as the church. One of these is the Bell public house, which is sixteenth-century and timber-framed. Next door are the associated weatherboarded stables.

In the locality: Claremont House, page 76; Claremont Landscape Garden, page 77; Kingston Museum, page 98; and church at Esher, page 70.

Egham
A small town situated close to the Thames, Egham has an attractive townscape but few old buildings. The lychgate of the church formed the porch of an earlier one. The nearby Katherine Wheel Hotel is a well-proportioned brick building. At the east end of the pedestrianised High Street is the King John sculpture set up in 1994. Further along are a Magna Carta fountain, also 1994, and a three-gabled Jacobean-style bank, built in 1896. Close by is the town museum in the Egham Literary Institute.

On the edge of the town are Runnymede with its associated memorials and the river Thames. To the west is Royal Holloway and Bedford New College, an enormous brick edifice. Built by Crossland, it was designed along the lines of a French palace. Today it is part of London University and can be seen from the A30.

Above left: *The King John sculpture in Egham.*
Above right: *The central tower of Royal Holloway and Bedford New College.*

South of Egham, a hotel and conference centre occupy the sixteenth-century Great Fosters. This five-gabled symmetrical brick building is surmounted by an attractive assembly of chimneys.

Egham Museum, page 95; **Picture Gallery**, page 95; **Runnymede**, page 109.

In the locality: Chertsey Museum, page 92; Great Cockrow Railway, page 108; Savill Garden, page 86; Spelthorne Museum, page 100; Staines Reservoir and Moor, page 58; Thorpe Park, page 109; Valley Garden, page 86; Virginia Water, page 59; and churches at Chertsey, page 68; and Thorpe, page 75.

Elstead

A village around a small green, Elstead lies beside the river Wey, which is crossed by a medieval bridge. Although containing few cottages of great importance, it makes an attractive whole, with its church and several inns. The village has a long association with the growing of carrots. Records of carrot growing date back to the sixteenth century and after the coming of the railways they were sent to Covent Garden by train from Milford.

To the east of Elstead is Fulbrook, a house designed by Lutyens. West of the village is Elstead Mill, now a restaurant. It once produced gold braid for officers' uniforms and, before that, worsted cloth. Beyond the mill is a nature reserve of the Surrey Wildlife Trust (SWT), set up to protect old water-meadows. The National Nature Reserve of Thursley Common and the SWT reserve at Bagmoor Common are also close by.

Thursley Common, page 59.

In the locality: Crooksbury Hill and Common, pages 51 and 62; Rural Life Centre, page 100; Soldiers' Ring earthwork, page 64; Waverley Abbey, page 87; Wey Valley bridges, page 106; and churches at Peper Harow, page 72; and Thursley, page 75.

Englefield Green

Savill Garden, page 86; Valley Garden, page 86.

Epsom

Market day Saturday.

The medieval village of Epsom began to grow considerably in the seventeenth century, when it became one of Britain's first spa towns. The original spa was developed after spring water on Epsom Common was found to contain sulphate of magnesium. The owner of the spring enclosed it and built a 'shed for the protection of invalids'. Within twenty years people were coming from all over Europe to take the waters. During the eighteenth century Epsom's popularity as a spa declined. Today, there are two reminders of this fashionable past. The well still remains, enclosed by iron railings at the end of Well Way. It is approached through a housing estate signposted 'The Wells' midway between Epsom and Ashtead on the A24. The other reminder is Waterloo House, some distance away in High Street. Near the roundabout at the west end, it is a large elegant building of 1690, now hidden behind a modern frontage. It housed the first assembly rooms to serve a spa anywhere and accommodated the fashionable visitors. In the early eighteenth century an apothecary named Levingstone opened a rival well. He too built assembly rooms close by. This is now numbers 126/132 and the Albion public house.

Soon after the establishment of the spa, Epsom Races started and the town became a residential area for city merchants. These three factors ensured that Epsom was richer in late Stuart, Queen Anne and Georgian houses than any other Surrey town. Some of these have survived following conversion into flats and offices, but many others have been demolished. Areas where some remain are Church Street, South Street and Woodcote. For vernacular architecture, the area to the west of High Street, at West Hill and Stamford Green, should be visited.

Most of the broad High Street is relatively modern. Almost opposite each other, however, near the clock-tower, are an eighteenth-century restaurant fronted by yew trees and a bow-windowed eighteenth-century chemist's shop.

A modern development is the stylish Ashley Centre. This is an airy shopping centre, with glass lifts and marble interior. The complex also contains a theatre.

Epsom Common, page 52; **Horton Country Park**, page 53; **Horton Park Children's Farm**, page 108.

In the locality: Bourne Hall Museum, page 95; Chessington World of Adventures, page 107; Galley Hills barrows, page 63; and church at Ashtead, page 66.

Esher

Esher is a small town with an attractive tree-lined High Street. At the north end, near Sandown Park racecourse, the large, early Victorian façade of the council offices hides a seventeenth-century building. A large green, just off the High Street, is surrounded by a varied selection of cottages and houses. Approached through a gateway, the Esher Place Estate comprises several streets of picturesque twentieth-century houses. At the end of Waynflete Tower Avenue, the red brick tower is all that remains of the fifteenth-century Esher Place, a house of Bishop Waynflete of Winchester.

Church of St George, page 70; **Claremont House**, page 76; **Claremont Landscape Garden**, page 77.

In the locality: Cobham Bus Museum, page 93; Painshill Park, page 83; and church at Cobham, page 69.

Ewell

There is evidence of human occupation at Ewell dating back to 20,000 BC. The springs which form the source of the Hogsmill River probably first attracted people to this village between Epsom and Sutton. The springs occur along the Thanet Sands which form a narrow belt between the chalk and the London Clay.

The Roman Stane Street passes through Ewell on its way from London to Chichester and the village may have been a staging post on this route. Later, at the time of Domesday, there is no mention of a church, although two mills were present.

The first major recorded event to have influenced the area was the building of the massive Nonsuch Palace by Henry VIII, on the site of the nearby village of Cuddington. By the time of his death the building, in the Tudor style similar to Hampton Court, was still incomplete. Work continued and the palace was to become one of the favourite residences of Elizabeth I. However, its popularity declined during the seventeenth century and it was demolished between 1682 and 1688. The site was excavated in 1959-61, but only a few stones remain, in Nonsuch Park. Nonsuch Mansion, built on the site for the Farmer family, was completed in 1806. It is a listed building and is often open on summer afternoons.

The greatest change to affect Ewell came with the development of suburbia in the 1930s. Until then Ewell had been a largely rural village, but as farmland was snapped up by developers it quickly changed, to become effectively part of south London. However, the village centre still retains many old buildings and an old world charm.

Bourne Hall Museum, page 95.

In the locality: Epsom Common, page 52; Galley Hills barrows, page 63; Horton Country Park, page 53; Horton Park Children's Farm, page 108; Whitehall, page 87.

Ewhurst

Ewhurst is beautifully set in the Wealden countryside between Cranleigh and Forest Green. Much of the country to the north is part of Hurtwood Control, allowing free access and spectacular views.

There was an important Roman villa and bath-house at Rapsley Farm, north of the village. This has been excavated and filled in, but at nearby Farley Heath the position of a Romano-British temple is marked out on the common.

The church is picturesque, sitting atop a small hill. Many of the houses around the village are large and attractive, being positioned in woodland settings. On a hill above the village a windmill has been converted into a dwelling.

Church of St Peter and St Paul, page 70; **Ewhurst Windmill**, page 103.

In the locality: Farley Heath Romano-British temple, page 63; Hurtwood Control, page 53; Leith Hill, page 54; church at Oakwoodhill, page 72.

Farleigh

Church of St Mary, page 70.

Farnham

Farnham, one of the finest Georgian towns in England, sits at the junction of the Roman road from London to Winchester and the older Pilgrims Way. The Saxons gave Farnham its name, which means ferny water-meadows', but its history goes back much further, even as far as the palaeolithic. Finds from this period have been made at Farnham, as have others from the mesolithic, neolithic, bronze and iron ages. Evidence of Romano-British occupation is scattered throughout Farnham,

St George's church, Esher.

largely related to the pottery industry. South of the river Wey, a small Saxon settlement was found in 1924.

By Domesday Farnham was wealthy and belonged to the Bishops of Winchester. The construction of the castle was followed by a deer park. In the first Civil War (1642-6) some fighting took place in Farnham, both sides using the castle as a base.

During the middle ages the market grew, as did the prosperity of the town, which was based on wheat and wool. Pottery manufacture recommenced during the sixteenth century and a new market house was commissioned. One hundred years later Farnham had one of the largest wheat markets in Britain. Wheat was replaced by hops in the eighteenth century. These were even more profitable, probably prompting much of the rebuilding which took place at that time.

Much of the Georgian architecture is to be found in Castle Street, West Street and Downing Street. Castle Street forms a perfect townscape, the broad market place being fringed with Georgian buildings and dominated by the castle. In West Street, opposite the end of Castle Street, is a beautiful Italianate building, now used as a bank. Many buildings were simply refronted, preserving much older structures behind their Georgian façades. Around the church are some attractive streets of terraced houses, such as Middle Church Lane and Vicarage Lane; Lower Church Lane is cobbled. The coming of the railway in 1849 made commuting to London possible and led to substantial development on the south side of the river, near the station.

The river Wey flows almost unnoticed through the town but is fringed with well-landscaped parks. Beyond the river, The Maltings, once an old brewery, is now a thriving arts centre. A wide range of events is held there, whilst upstairs is an exhibition gallery. Not far away, in Waggon Yard, is the New Ashgate Gallery. More exhibitions are staged at West Surrey College of Art and Design, one of Britain's leading art colleges. William Cobbett, author of *Rural Rides*, was born in the pub which bears his name, close to The Maltings. Bourne Mill in Guildford Road, is also of interest.

Church of St Andrew, page 70; **Farnham Castle**, page 78; **Museum of Farnham**, page 95.

In the locality: Birdworld, page 107; Blackwater Valley Visitor Centre, page 107; Crooksbury Hill and Common, pages 51 and 62; Frensham Country Park, page 52; Hogs Back Brewery, page 108; Rowhill Copse, page 58; Rural Life Centre, page 100; Soldiers' Ring earthwork, page 64; Waverley Abbey, page 87.

Fetcham

Bocketts Farm Park, page 107; church of St Mary, page 70.

Frensham

Frensham Common bowl barrows, page 63; Frensham Country Park, page 52.

Friday Street

Friday Street is an isolated hamlet set next to a lake in a steep wooded valley. It can be approached only by steep, single-track lanes, between high sandstone banks. These lanes once ran level with the top of the banks, but the iron wheels of carts cut deeply into the sandstone for centuries until the lanes were surfaced and pneumatic tyres invented.

There is a short street of cottages by the lakeside, which ends in woodland. The public house here, the Stephen Langton, is named after the Archbishop of Canterbury who was the first witness to the king's seal on Magna Carta. Many legends have grown up around him as a result of a novel by Martin Tupper, who lived at Albury, but Langton had no connection with the area.

Footpaths traverse the woods around Friday Street, leading towards Leith Hill and other local beauty spots. Water birds such as mallard, coot, moorhen and heron can be spotted on the lake and along the associated river Tillingbourne.

In the locality: Abinger pit dwelling, page 62; Holmbury hillfort, page 64; Hurtwood Control, page 53; Leith Hill, page 54; church at Abinger, page 66.

Frimley

Blackwater Valley Visitor Centre, page 107; church of St Peter, page 70; Frimley Aqueduct, page 103.

West Street, Farnham.

Godalming

The first mention of Godalming is in the will of Alfred, about AD 880. The name is most likely of Saxon origin, meaning 'people of Godhelm'. By Domesday, in 1086, the settlement was relatively wealthy. During the middle ages it became a market centre, receiving a grant of a market charter and annual fair in 1300. By the sixteenth century it had grown into a thriving centre of the cloth trade. In 1749 the opening of the Portsmouth turnpike placed Godalming on an important through route. In 1881 the town became the first in the world to have a public electricity supply.

Godalming is a town full of fascinating buildings and narrow streets. An excellent starting point for a tour is The Pepperpot, or Old Town Hall, opposite the local museum. Along Mill Lane, the left-hand portion of the Red Lion was the original grammar school. Further on, the Little Fort was built by two Jacobite sisters of General Oglethorpe, as a defence in case of siege.

Opposite The Pepperpot in High Street is a timbered building dating from 1570, formerly a coaching inn. Opposite Moss Lane is a tall narrow building, with remains of a hoist. This was previously a wool merchant's warehouse. Crown Court formerly consisted of sixteenth-century clothworkers' cottages but they became dilapidated and were demolished; the materials were used to construct the present dignified car park entrance. Opposite Hart's Yard, numbers 74-6 and 80 retain some beautiful brickwork in their upper storeys.

Between the parish church and the river are the delightful Phillips Memorial Cloisters, which commemorate the wireless operator on the *Titanic* and were restored in 1994. Near the Town Bridge was Godalming Wharf, marking the end of the Godalming Navigation. The canal is owned by the National Trust and has been the scene of narrowboat rallies. Across the river from the town are some meadows known as the Lammas Lands.

On a hill above the town stand the majestic buildings of Charterhouse School, which moved here in 1872 from London. The style is Gothic, but the building material is local Bargate stone.

Godstone pond and village green.

Godalming Museum, page 95; **church of St Peter and St Paul**, page 70; **Wey Navigation Canal**, page 60.

In the locality: Busbridge Lakes Waterfowl and Gardens, page 107; Loseley House, page 82; Oakhurst Cottage, page 83; Shalford Mill, page 105; Thursley Common, page 59; Watts Gallery, page 93; Winkworth Arboretum, page 90; Witley Common, page 60; churches at Compton, page 69; Dunsfold, page 69; Hascombe, page 71; Peper Harow, page 72; Witley, page 75.

Godstone

In contrast to the nearby street village of Blechingley, Godstone is a perfect example of a village built around a large green. At one corner of the tree-lined green is a small pond inhabited by ducks. As well as the cottages surrounding the green, there are three old public houses here. The White Hart and Godstone hotels are both sixteenth-century. The Bell is largely eighteenth-century but has older parts behind.

A path alongside the White Hart leads past Bay Pond, a nature reserve owned by the Surrey Wildlife Trust. At the far end of this path are the parish church and a street of cottages, known as Church Town. Next to the church are picturesque almshouses, built in 1872 by George Gilbert Scott. Opposite, there are several other attractive cottages.

Godstone is situated in an area of high-quality sands which have been extensively quarried. To the north of the village green, behind some cottages, two old quarries are now flooded, forming emergency reservoirs and a nature reserve.

Godstone Farm, page 108.

In the locality: East Surrey Museum, page 91; churches at Blechingley, page 67; Oxted, page 72; and Tandridge, page 74.

Gomshall

Gomshall Mill, page 104; Hackhurst Local Nature Reserve, page 53.

Great Bookham

Bookham Common, page 50; church of St Nicholas, page 70.

Guildford

Market days Friday and Saturday.

Guildford, county town of Surrey, is a bustling place set in a steep-sided gap in the North

Downs, carved by the river Wey. Its steep High Street, paved with setts, lined by historic buildings and with glimpses of the Downs, is one of the most attractive streets in England.

No prehistoric or Roman finds have yet come to light from the historic core of Guildford. Despite its important position controlling a gap through the North Downs, there is no significant archaeological evidence earlier than Saxon times. On Guildown, the hill visible from the High Street, more than two hundred graves were found in 1928, thirty-five of which belonged to the late sixth century.

Around AD 900 Guildford was mentioned in the will of Alfred the Great, the first documentary record of the town. At this time a church probably stood on the site of St Mary's. By the end of the tenth century Guildford had its own mint. During the eleventh century the massive motte on which the castle keep stands was thrown up.

Off Castle Hill the blocked entrances to early medieval chalk mines can be seen, by the steps to Racks Close. From here a hard vein of chalk, or clunch, was extracted, for use as a building stone in the town. The prosperity of this medieval town, which then covered an area between the castle and the friary, was derived from the wool trade. Racks Close was named from the racks on which Guildford blue cloth was dried, following its dyeing with woad.

In the middle ages a Dominican friary stood on the site of the present Friary shopping complex. This was later replaced by a house, a barracks and then a brewery. Archaeologists uncovered the remains of the friary before construction of the present building began. Information about this and other parts of Guildford is presented in the museum in Quarry Street.

The High Street contains a large number of historic buildings. Starting from the top, beyond the section paved with setts, there is the Tudor grammar school. Set around a quadrangle, this school, founded in 1509, contains a rare chained library.

Further down, opposite Holy Trinity Church, is the Hospital of the Blessed Trinity, founded in 1619 by George Abbot, a local man who had become Archbishop of Canterbury. These almshouses are arranged around an internal courtyard which is approached through a splendid gatehouse. Abbot's statue is at the top of the High Street.

A little further down the hill, an attractive clock projects over the street from the historic Guildhall. This Tudor building was refronted in 1683, when it gained its present elegant balcony. A few yards away stands Guildford House, dating to 1660 and now used as an art gallery. Almost opposite is Tunsgate, an imposing nineteenth-century structure originally created as a corn market. It was last used as such in 1901. It has been altered to allow traffic to pass between the columns.

North Street, which runs parallel to High Street, contains some modern buildings like the Post Office and also has the town's street market. Between North Street and High Street are many narrow streets lined with specialist shops. In one of these passages can be found the Angel Hotel, a coaching inn of the seventeenth and nineteenth centuries. It retains its coaching yard, wooden gallery and a thirteenth-century vaulted basement.

The river Wey, which provides the spectacular setting for Guildford, is strangely hidden in the town. It was one of the earliest canalised rivers in England, being opened as far as Guildford in 1653. The Godalming Navigation is the most southerly part of Britain's canal network. The first lock on the canal is to be found behind Mill Mead. Near the town bridge is a treadmill crane. A short distance away, on an island in the river, is the Yvonne Arnaud Theatre.

There are many other places to see in Guildford including St Mary's church in Quarry Street and The Chestnuts, where Lewis Carroll died, in Castle Hill (private). There are two sculptures in Guildford to his character Alice: one, showing her peering through the looking glass, is in the castle grounds; the other, of Alice and the rabbit, is on the lawns at Mill Mead.

On Stag Hill stands the modern Cathedral of the Holy Spirit, built between 1936 and 1966 in simplified Gothic style. Nearby is the expanding University of Surrey, first opened in 1966.
Brooking Architectural Museum Trust, page 95; **Cathedral of the Holy Spirit**, page

'Alice and the rabbit' at Millmead, Guild-
ford, and, below, The Chestnuts, Castle Hill,
Guildford, where Lewis Carroll died.

70; **Chantries**, page 51; **church of Holy Trinity**, page 70; **church of St Mary**, page 71; **Guildford Castle**, page 79; **Guildford Crane and Treadmill**, page 104; **Guildford House Gallery**, page 97; **Guildford Museum**, page 97; **Guildhall**, page 97; **Town Mill**, page 106; **University of Surrey Library Gallery**, page 97; **Wey Navigation Canal**, page 60.

In the locality: Albury Park, page 76; Blackheath, page 50; British Red Cross Museum and Archives, page 101; Burpham Court Farm Park, page 107; Chilworth Gunpowder Mills, page 103; Clandon Park, page 76; Gomshall Mill, page 104; Hatchlands, page 80; Loseley House, page 82; Newlands Corner, page 55; Newlands Corner round barrow, page 64; the Old Farm at Shere, page 109; Ripley Local History Museum, page 100; Shalford Mill, page 105; Shere Museum, page 100; Watts Gallery, page 93; churches at Albury Park, page 66; Chilworth, page 68; Compton, page 69; Puttenham, page 72; Shere, page 73; Wanborough, page 75; Worplesdon, page 75.

Ham

Ham House, page 80.

Hambledon
Oakhurst Cottage, page 83.

Hascombe
Church of St Peter, page 71; Hascombe hillfort, page 63.

Haslemere
The first mention of Haslemere was made about 1180, when it was part of the manor of Godalming. It seems that an early settlement may have existed at Haste Hill, to the southeast, but the town existed in its present position by the thirteenth century. Its appearance as a market centre in 1221 has led to suggestions that it may have been a planted town, like Reigate. Haslemere is based on a T-shaped plan, the High Street broadening out to the south to form the market place. The market must have been a centre for the woollen trade during the middle ages, until its decline towards the end of the sixteenth century.

An interesting walk around the town can be made, starting from the Educational Museum at the north end of the High Street. As one walks towards the early nineteenth-century Old Town Hall, several Queen Anne and Georgian buildings will be passed, interspersed with the occasional one of sixteenth-century construction. As one turns left into Petworth Road, a group of buildings of the sixteenth and seventeenth centuries may be seen. On one's return past the Old Town Hall, Lower Street has an interesting group of cottages along the High Pavement. A little further on the left stands the Congregational chapel of 1791.

Above Lower Street, Shepherd's Hill contains a group of cottages listed for their historic interest. Anderson Court was the first cottage hospital in the town. Back in Lower Street, Sheepskin House was once used for skinning and the curing of furs. Nearby is Tanners Lane, where a rich tanner named Bradford lived. Beyond Tanners Lane and the railway bridge lies Church Green. Here there are three buildings of interest: Church Hill House, a beautiful Queen Anne building; Church Hill Gate, built in 1589; and the parish church of St Bartholomew.

Haslemere is on the border of Surrey, West Sussex and Hampshire and is surrounded by beautiful countryside, protected by the National Trust. Included in this land is Blackdown, Marley Common, Waggoners Wells and the Devil's Punchbowl. One of three founders of the National Trust, Sir Robert Hunter, lived in Haslemere.

Educational Museum, page 97.

In the locality: Devil's Punchbowl, page 52; churches at Chiddingfold, page 68; Thursley, page 75; and Witley, page 75.

Haxted
Haxted Mill, page 98.

Headley
Headley Heath, page 53; Nower Wood, page 56.

Hindhead
Over 800 feet (245 metres) above sea level, on the edge of the Devil's Punchbowl, sits Hindhead. It is largely a residential area amid pine woods but there is also a small group of shops around a crossroads on the A3. One of the most interesting buildings is the Royal Huts Hotel, an old coaching inn. Hindhead, like Haslemere, is surrounded by much open countryside owned by the National Trust. In the bottom of the Devil's Punchbowl, a large basin-like valley around the rim of which curves the A3, are some old cottages and an isolated youth hostel.

Devil's Punchbowl, page 52.

In the locality: Educational Museum, page 97; Frensham Country Park, page 52; Thursley Common, page 59; church at Thursley, page 75.

Holmbury St Mary
Holmbury hillfort, page 64.

Horley
A growing town situated on the West Sussex border, Horley is largely a mixture of Victorian and modern architecture, centred on a crossroads. The town owes its origins to the coming of the Brighton railway. Despite appearances, the attractive weatherboarded Foresters' Arms in Victoria Road probably

dates from the late nineteenth century. More recently Horley has expanded further, thanks to its proximity to Gatwick Airport.

In the locality: Gatwick Zoo, page 108; Lowfield Heath Windmill, page 104; Outwood Common Windmill, page 105; Providence Chapel (Charlwood), page 68; churches at Burstow, page 67; Charlwood, page 68; and Outwood, page 72.

Kew
Royal Botanic Gardens, page 84.

Kingston upon Thames
Market days Monday to Saturday.
Although now part of Greater London, Kingston has always looked towards Surrey. Even today, Surrey County Hall is situated in the town. Human occupation of the area has continued for many centuries, and Kingston was always an important crossing point of the Thames. The early bridge, in place by 1193, was the first bridge above London until 1750; it was just north of the present bridge. At Kingston seven West Saxon kings were crowned and these events are marked by the Coronation Stone, a shapeless piece of grey sandstone, enclosed by some Victorian railings outside the county court. It has been moved several times from its original position. Very close by is the late twelfth-century Clattern Bridge, spanning the Hogsmill with three arches.

The remains of old Kingston are grouped around the Market Place, which has at its centre the Victorian Market House. In the triangular market place surrounding this Italianate building a street market is held regularly. The area is surrounded by a range of buildings varying in date from the sixteenth to twentieth centuries. Behind the Market House, Boots is an amazing building, created in 1909. Its front is a jumble of timbering, plasterwork, statues and heraldry. There are several buildings in the surrounding streets, including number 9 Harrow Passage, dating to about 1530. Church Street, Crown Passage, Applemarket and the west end of Eden Street are all worthy of attention.

Most of central Kingston is a modern shopping centre, with the Thames well hidden. Only on the approach from Esher does the road follow the riverside. There are pleasant walks along the south bank of the river to Richmond, and along the north bank to Hampton Court. Both start from Kingston Bridge.

Kingston Museum, page 98.

In the locality: Claremont House, page 76; Claremont Landscape Garden, page 77; Ham House, page 80; Richmond Park, page 57; churches at Esher, page 70; Petersham, page 72.

Laleham
Church of All Saints, page 71.

Leatherhead
Once a small market town, Leatherhead has been much modernised. An attractive modern shopping centre has been built, along with a new clock-tower. The town is also the home

One of Nuthall's gazebos at Kingston upon Thames.

of the Thorndike Theatre, where many plays are premiered before moving to the West End. Wesley is said to have preached his last sermon under a cedar tree which used to stand in front of Wesley House, at the top of Bull Hill.

The church of St Mary is one of the most interesting buildings in the town. In Bridge Street, the Running Horse public house is worth a visit. This is a rambling timber-framed building, partly dating from the fifteenth century and believed to have been described in a poem by Henry VIII's tutor, John Skelton, in 1517. In Gravel Hill are Sweech House and several other old cottages. The museum is set in a restored seventeenth-century cottage in Church Street.

Church of St Mary and St Nicholas, page 71; **Leatherhead Museum of Local History**, page 98.

In the locality: Bocketts Farm Park, page 107; Bookham Commons, page 50; Chapel Farm and Animal Trail, page 107; Chessington World of Adventures, page 107; Cobham Bus Museum, page 93; Cobham Mill, page 103; Headley Heath, page 53; Norbury Park, page 55; Nower Wood, page 56; Painshill Park, page 83; Polesden Lacey, page 83; churches at Ashtead, page 66; Cobham, page 69; Fetcham, page 70; Great Bookham, page 70; Mickleham, page 72; Ockham, page 72; Stoke D'Abernon, page 74; West Horsley, page 75.

Leigh

A rambling medieval timbered house with a Horsham-stone roof faces the weatherboarded village pub across Leigh green. Other old cottages, the church and village pump add to the attractive scene. Along the road to the north stands Leigh Place, a Gothick-style house surrounded by a moat. Large oak trees line the lanes around this village, which is pronounced 'Lie'

Lightwater

Lightwater Country Park, page 54.

Limpsfield

Another attractive street village, Limpsfield is surrounded by wooded Wealden countryside. As well as The Chart and Limpsfield Common, there are attractive walks to be followed in Titsey Park, north of the village, at the end of Water Lane.

The village street, which narrows at the south end, is a delightful mixture of vernacular buildings ranging from the fifteenth century to the twentieth. Many of the pavements are constructed from brick and local ironstone. Detillens is well positioned among the small shops and cottages, which house a range of small businesses. At the end of the village, in Titsey Road, Old Court Cottage is a Grade II listed building incorporating a medieval aisled hall.

Limpsfield Chart and Common, page 55.

In the locality: Beaver Waterworld and Reptile Zoo, page 107; Kent/Surrey border cross-valley dyke, page 64; churches at Oxted, page 72; Tandridge, page 74; and Tatsfield, page 74.

Lingfield

Lingfield is a large village, best known for its racecourse. However, the area around the church has been designated a conservation area and includes a fine selection of buildings of the sixteenth to eighteenth centuries. A plan, showing the age of each building, is affixed to a wall.

A short walk away, in the main street, may be found the cross and village cage. The cage, built as the village lock-up in 1773, was last used in 1882, to hold a poacher.

Nothing remains of the college founded by Sir Reginald Cobham in 1431, except for the Old Guest House, now the library. This is a fifteenth-century hall-house. Nearby, a fine eighteenth century farmhouse called The College marks the site of the original establishment.

Church of St Peter and St Paul, page 71.

In the locality: Greathed Manor, page 79; Haxted Mill, page 98; London Temple Visitors' Centre, page 72; church at Crowhurst, page 69.

Littleton

Church of St Mary Magdalene, page 71.

Lower Kingswood

Church of Jesus Christ the Wisdom of God, page 71.

The cage or old village lock-up at Lingfield.

Lyne

Merstham

Mickleham

Mitcham

Morden

Mytchett

Newchapel

Newdigate

Oakwoodhill

Ockham

Ockley
Surrounding an enormous green, with Stane Street, a former Roman road, along one side, Ockley has a charm unique in Surrey. Stane Street is now the A29 and appears to be lined by a selection of public houses. The green is irregular in shape, varying from about 50 yards (46 metres) to 200 yards (184 metres) in width. The cottages around it are a pleasant mixture of weatherboarding, brick and tile, in a wide variety of styles. There is a large pond on the green, as well as a cricket square, making this a good place to spend a Sunday afternoon. Ockley Court is hidden behind a wall opposite the church, north-east of the green. It is an eighteenth-century brick building, with two bow windows. Jayes Park, to the west of Ockley, has an interesting group of barns, well preserved.

Cottages near the church at Blechingley.

Brockham village, looking across the green.

Invading Danes suffered a severe defeat at a place recorded as Aclea in 851, where they met Ethelwulf's army. Some people have identified this as Ockley, but there is no proof that the battle took place here.

In the locality: Ewhurst Windmill, page 103; Leith Hill, page 54; Vann Lake, page 59; churches at Ewhurst, page 70; Oakwoodhill, page 72.

Old Woking
Church of St Peter, page 72.

Outwood
Church of St John the Baptist, page 72; Outwood Common Windmill, page 105.

Oxted
Oxted is divided into two parts. Old Oxted is one hilly street south of the A25, lined with timber-framed buildings mostly dating from the sixteenth century. At the crossroads near the top of the hill is the large timber-framed Old Bell public house, with a jettied upper storey.

To the north of the A25 lies the present-day town of Oxted, largely a twentieth-century creation, following the coming of the railway. The shopping centre is split in two by the railway line and contains some of the most spectacular fake timber-framing to be seen in the south of England. Nearly all the buildings are in this style, including the cinema. The slope of the eastern street adds to the effect, making the town worth a visit just for the novelty. On the edge of the town can be found the ancient church of St Mary and nearby is one of the few working chalk quarries remaining in this area.

Church of St Mary, page 72.

In the locality: Beaver Waterworld and Reptile Zoo, page 107; Godstone Farm, page 108; Haxted Mill, page 98; Limpsfield Chart and Common, page 55; Staffhurst Wood, page 58; churches at Crowhurst, page 69; Tandridge, page 74; and Tatsfield, page 74.

Peper Harow
Church of St Nicholas, page 72.

Petersham
Church of St Peter, page 72.

Purley
In Saxon times 'Purley' was an open space in woodland with pear trees. However, today it is largely a suburban area, becoming part of the London Borough of Croydon in 1965. Like all places in this area, its development was much influenced by the coming of the railway in 1841. Before this, Purley had the distinction of having had, in 1804, an early smallpox vaccination session for nine poor Coulsdon children, at the Rose and Crown. Reedham owes its name to an orphanage, founded by the Reverend Andrew Reed in 1844 and demolished in 1980 because of a lack of orphans. At the beginning of the twentieth century William Webb pioneered his garden village concept at West Purley.

In the locality: Croydon Clocktower, page 94; Croydon Old Palace, page 78; East Surrey Museum, page 91; Surrey Iron Railway, page 105; churches at Caterham, page 67; Coulsdon, page 69; and Croydon, page 69.

Puttenham
Puttenham is a delightful street village, on the edge of the chalk below the Hog's Back. The cottages are a mixture of chalk, sandstone and brick. In the centre of the village is a small gallery.

South of the church, Puttenham Priory is a five-bay stuccoed house of 1762. It has a central three-bay pediment, supported by fluted capitals and is one of the few fine Palladian houses in Surrey.

The eighteenth-century weatherboarded barns of Greys Home Farm, also near the church, are perhaps one of the best groups of buildings in Puttenham. There are many other interesting buildings, including Hurlands. Built in 1898, it was the last country house by Philip Webb.

Church of St John the Baptist, page 72; **Puttenham Common**, page 56.

In the locality: Crooksbury Hill and Common, pages 51 and 62; Watts Gallery, page 93; churches at Compton, page 69; Peper Harow, page 72; and Wanborough, page 75.

Pyrford
Church of St Nicholas, page 73; Newark Priory, page 82.

Reigate Old Town Hall and (right) the statue of Margot Fonteyn by London Road.

Ranmore

Church of St Barnabas, page 73.

Redhill

Like Woking, Redhill is a largely Victorian railway town, much modernised. Before the coming of the railway to Brighton in 1841, it was nothing more than a small hamlet. By the end of the century it had overtaken neighbouring Reigate in size. Since the 1960s much modernisation has taken place, leading to the elimination of much of Redhill's Victorian character. Today, the heart of the town comprises a modern shopping centre, theatre and office buildings.

The area is important for its deposits of fuller's earth. There has been a long history of extensive quarrying at Nutfield, just outside the town. Many of the old quarries are now flooded, making ideal areas for birdwatching. Some of the area forms a small country park.

Royal Earlswood Hospital Museum, page 99.

In the locality: Fire Brigades of Surrey Preservation Trust, page 99; Outwood Common Windmill, page 105; Reigate Heath Windmill, page 105; Reigate Priory Museum, page 99; Surrey Iron Railway, page 105; Wray Common Windmill, page 106; churches at Blechingley, page 67; Merstham, page 71; Outwood, page 72; and Reigate, page 73.

Reigate

Implements dating back to the bronze age have been found in the area and the manor was recorded as Churchefelle in Domesday, when it was centred around the church of St Mary Magdalene, to the east of the town. A castle was built around 1100 to the north of the present High Street, the new town of Reigate being established alongside in the twelfth century. All that remains are the earthworks in the Castle Grounds, which are laid out as attractive gardens and can be reached by a flight of steps between the shops. During the Civil War the castle was held first

Pippbrook House, Dorking, is now the County Library.

The Phillips Memorial Cloisters in Godalming commemorate the wireless operator on the 'Titanic'.

The parish church of St Andrew at Farnham.

by the Royalists, then the Parliamentarians. Afterwards it fell into disrepair. The castle gateway was built when the grounds were restored in 1777. Beneath the grounds is the Baron's Cave. It is not known when or why it was built, but it was an important feature of the castle. Open days are held regularly and visits can be arranged by telephoning 01737 241179.

Reigate Priory was an Augustinian monastery founded by the Earl of Surrey in the early thirteenth century. After the Dissolution of the Monasteries, the priory was converted into a Palladian mansion, which is now a school. The building contains a particularly fine staircase and fireplace, as well as a recently updated museum. Surrounding the school is Priory Park, open to the public and comprising a large expanse of parkland and woodland with a lake. An annual festival and firework display are held each September in the park and around the town.

High Street and Bell Street, both a sympathetic blend of old and new buildings, meet Tunnel Road at the Old Town Hall of 1728. This attractive arcaded building stands in a commanding position in the town by the tunnel, which was cut through the castle mound in 1824 and once provided an unusual entrance to Reigate. A walk through the tunnel leads to a modern office development, by which stands a statue of the ballerina Margot Fonteyn, who was born in the town.

Old buildings can be found in a number of streets including Slipshoe Street, Nutley Lane and Upper West Street. There are windmills nearby at Reigate Heath and Wray Common.
Church of St Mary Magdalene, page 73; **Fire Brigades of Surrey Preservation Trust**, page 99; **Reigate Heath barrows**, page 64; **Reigate Heath Windmill**, page 105; **Reigate Priory Museum**, page 99; **Wray Common Windmill**, page 106.

In the locality: Betchworth Chalk Quarries, page 102; Royal Earlswood Hospital Museum, page 99; Surrey Iron Railway, page 105; churches at Betchworth, page 66; Lower Kingswood, page 71; and Merstham, page 71.

Richmond-upon-Thames

Since prehistoric times the river Thames has attracted settlement in the Richmond area.

There have been finds from Ham Fields; a neolithic site was found at Twickenham and an axe hoard at Teddington. There are also possible bronze age and Roman burials in the district.

The area's royal palaces ensured Richmond became a fashionable centre for writers, actors, poets, painters and statesmen. When the railway came to Richmond during the nineteenth century, there was a growth in the population, but the wealth of the residents allowed the elegant character of the former village to be maintained. In the Victorian era the town became a fashionable river resort, a position it has maintained ever since. The town is also a major shopping centre with a good range of speciality shops.

Behind George Street is the lovely Richmond Green, one of the best in England. On one corner is the Richmond Theatre, built of brown terracotta and brick in 1899. It is surmounted by two symmetrical turrets with copper-covered cupolas. The tree-lined green is surrounded by a large variety of seventeenth- and eighteenth-century houses. On the southwest side is Maids of Honour Row, which was built in 1724 for the maids of honour of Caroline of Anspach, George II's queen, who lived at Kew.

Nearby stand the remains of Richmond Palace. Little survives, but a simple gateway, built during the reign of Henry VII, faces the green. Through this gateway one enters Old Palace Yard, where Old Palace, Palace Gate House and The Wardrobe incorporate parts of the old buildings. The secluded courtyard also contains several other attractive but far more recent buildings. Through the courtyard is Old Palace Lane, running down to the river, and lined with a terrace of nineteenth-century cottages. At the corner, facing the Thames, is the Palladian-style Asgill House, built on the site of the palace brewhouse in 1757-8.

Hill Street leads out of the town towards Petersham. A branch off to the left climbs the famous Richmond Hill, from where there are spectacular views of the Thames.

The Thames towpath provides exhilarating walks, as do nearby Richmond Park and Petersham Meadows. From the quayside it is possible to catch a boat to Kingston, Hampton

The modern river terrace at Richmond-upon-Thames.

Court, Teddington, Kew, Putney and West-minster. On the riverside north of the town is Kew Gardens. Details of walking tours of Richmond can be obtained from the tourist information centre.

Richmond was part of Surrey until 1965, when it was combined with Twickenham, previously in Middlesex, to form the present London borough. The part of the borough north of the Thames is outside the scope of this book but includes a number of places worth visiting, while in the area. These include Orleans House Gallery, Hampton Court Palace and Park, Marble Hill House and Park, York House, Strawberry Hill House, Syon Park and Bushy Park.

Museum of Richmond, page 100; **Richmond Park**, page 57.

In the locality: Ham House, page 80; Kingston Museum, page 98; Royal Botanic Gardens, page 84; church at Petersham, page 72.

Ripley

Ripley Local History Museum, page 100.

Shalford

Shalford Mill, page 105.

Shepperton

The church of St Nicholas is attractively placed at the head of a square, bordered by eighteenth-century houses and The Rectory. Although The Rectory appears to be built of brick, it is faced with mathematical tiles, which look exactly like bricks. They conceal a fifteenth-century hall-house.

At Shepperton Lock, the river Wey and the Wey Navigation join the Thames. The Eyot is an island in the Thames here, the alternative name of which is D'Oyly Carte Island. The father of Rupert D'Oyly Carte once hoped to build an annexe of the Savoy Hotel here. Later, he decided to live there himself.

Church of St Nicholas, page 73.

In the locality: Brooklands Museum, page 100; Elmbridge Museum, page 101; churches at Chertsey, page 68; Laleham, page 71; and Littleton, page 71.

Guildford Cathedral from the east.

Reigate Priory, once the home of Lord Howard of Effingham, now houses a school and a museum.

The river Tillingbourne at Shere.

Shere

Said by some to be England's prettiest village, Shere is situated on the river Tillingbourne, between the North Downs and the Greensand Hills.

Upper Street and Middle Street are lined by cottages, many dating to the seventeenth century. These are built of various materials including wattle and daub, brick and flint. Timber framing is a feature of the village.

In Lower Street stands the Old Prison, a small two-storey timber-framed house probably built in the seventeenth century. Its front wing was used as the local lock-up. It retains a barred, unglazed window.

The Square has some pleasing buildings, with St James's church at its head. Among them is High House, built of brick in the English bond during the sixteenth century. Just off The Square is the museum.

The river Tillingbourne flows through the centre of the village, making a picturesque ford in Lower Street. To the north, near the bypass, stands the Manor House, built by Reginald Bray about 1844. A bridge across Upper Street links the house to its kitchen garden on the other side of the road.

Church of St James, page 73; **Shere Museum**, page 100; **The Old Farm at Shere**, page 109.

In the locality: Albury Park, page 76; Blackheath, page 50; Chilworth Gunpowder Mills, page 103; Gomshall Mill, page 104; Hackhurst Local Nature Reserve, page 53; Hurtwood Control, page 53; Newlands Corner, page 55; Newlands Corner round barrow, page 64; Shalford Mill, page 105; Silent Pool, page 58; churches at Abinger, page 66; Albury Park, page 66; Chilworth, page 68; and Wotton, page 75.

Staines

Market days Wednesday and Saturday.
Situated a few miles south of Heathrow Airport and close to the M25, Staines is an important communications centre, and the High Street and attractive bridge over the Thames are often clogged with traffic.

The main street is a pleasant mix of buildings, but none is exceptional. As a whole, however, they form a well-balanced townscape. In Market Square, housed in an old fire station, is the local museum.

Occupation of the Staines area goes back to a causewayed enclosure of neolithic times, discovered by aerial photography. From Roman times until the fifteenth century, Staines was an important crossing point of the Thames and the area near the river was a Roman town.

The White Horse in the centre of Shere village.

The oldest remaining part of Staines is to be seen in Church Street and Binbury Row. Here most of the buildings date between the seventeenth and nineteenth centuries. Evidence of Georgian and Victorian buildings can be found in the upper storeys of many shops in the town centre, where modern fronts have been added at street level. Staines West station (now closed) is one of the few railway stations to have been converted from a house. A town trail, giving details of buildings of interest in the town, can be obtained from the museum.

Spelthorne Museum, page 100; **Staines Reservoir and Moor**, page 58.

In the locality: Chertsey Museum, page 92; Egham Museum, page 95; Picture Gallery (Royal Holloway College), page 95; Runnymede, page 109; Savill Garden, page 86; Thorpe Park, page 109; Valley Garden, page 86; churches at Chertsey, page 68; Laleham, page 71; Littleton, page 71; Shepperton, page 73; Stanwell, page 74; Thorpe, page 75.

Stanwell
Church of St Mary, page 74.

Stoke D'Abernon
Church of St Mary, page 74.

Sunbury
Formerly a Thames-side village, Sunbury still has a sprinkling of villas around its old centre by the river. The largest of these is the brick Palladian Sunbury Court, now used by the Salvation Army. Between this building and the church are several more large houses, mostly eighteenth-century in date.

Sunbury is said by many to be the site where Oliver Twist and Bill Sykes slept beneath a yew tree, before the Shepperton robbery, in the Dickens novel.

In the locality: churches at Laleham, page 71; Littleton, page 71; and Shepperton, page 73.

Sunningdale
Sunningdale bowl barrow, page 65.

Sutton
Since about 1850 Sutton has expanded to become largely a commuter area for London.

It still fulfils a mainly residential function, having the dubious distinction of only four listed buildings. There are, however, numerous Victorian houses of all sizes. Also, there is a theatre converted from a church, a mile-long shopping street and one of the finest libraries in Europe.

In the locality: Bourne Hall Museum, page 95; Carew Manor and Dovecote, page 76; Carshalton Heritage Centre, page 91; Croydon Old Palace, page 78; Croydon Clocktower, page 94; Deen City Farm, page 108; Little Holland House, page 82; Wandle Industrial Museum, page 99; Whitehall, page 87; churches at Beddington, page 66; Carshalton, page 67; and Croydon, page 69.

Tandridge
Church of St Peter, page 74.

Tatsfield
Beaver Waterworld and Reptile Zoo, page 107; church of St Mary, page 74.

Thames Ditton
The area around the church still retains some image of a riverside village, despite surrounding development. Although Thames Ditton still has an attractive appearance, much of the village economy has gone, with farms being turned into private homes and their land built over. The large Georgian house near the church used to be Boyle Farm.

In nearby Hinchley Wood, Telegraph Lane is named after the three-storey semaphore tower, built around 1820. It was one of a series stretching from Whitehall to Portsmouth, used by the Admiralty to send signals to their ships.

In the locality: Claremont House, page 76; Claremont Landscape Garden, page 77; Kingston Museum, page 98; church at Esher, page 70.

Thorpe
Church of St Mary, page 75; Thorpe Park, page 109.

Thursley
Thursley is dominated by the common, now a National Nature Reserve, which reaches right

The Barley Mow by the green at Tilford.

to the edge of the village. There is no village centre, but there are some very attractive cottages, mainly along two cul-de-sacs running south. Lutyens converted a row of cottages into a house called The Corner, when he was only nineteen. The Lane contains sixteenth-century Olde Hall with a rubble centre and timber-framed ends. Other cottages here are of brick or are tile-hung. There are many other interesting buildings in the village of dates between the sixteenth and eighteenth centuries. Prospect Cottage was built in 1900 by Lutyens, as the village hall.

Church of St Michael and All Angels, page 75; **Thursley Common**, page 59.

In the locality: Devil's Punchbowl, page 52; Witley Common, page 60.

Tilford

Two medieval bridges cross the river Wey at this attractive village just south-east of Farnham. The picturesque triangular village green is the scene of cricket matches in the summer and on it stands the magnificent King's Oak, probably over eight hundred years old.

Rural Life Centre, page 100.

Tongham

Hogs Back Brewery, page 108.

Virginia Water

Virginia Water, page 59.

Walliswood

Wallis Wood, page 60.

Walton-on-Thames

The current Walton Bridge at the end of New Zealand Avenue is the fourth on the site since the first wooden bridge was opened in 1750. From the bridge there are pleasant towpath walks, passing the course of Sunbury Regatta.

Perhaps the most interesting building in Walton is the Old Manor House, in Manor Road, parts of which date from the sixteenth

Above: *The lake at Friday Street.*

Right: *Silent Pool, near Shere, where King John is supposed to have come across a young girl bathing.*

century. It is said to have been the home of Judge Jeffreys in the late seventeenth century.

In the locality: Brooklands Museum, page 100; Chertsey Museum, page 92; Claremont House, page 76; Claremont Landscape Garden, page 77; Cobham Bus Museum, page 93; Cobham Mill, page 103; Elmbridge Museum, page 101; Painshill Park, page 83; churches at Cobham, page 69; Esher, page 70; Laleham, page 71; Shepperton, page 73; Whiteley Village, page 75.

Wanborough
Church of St Bartholomew, page 75.

Warlingham
Warlingham village green is now a public garden, surrounded by busy roads. At the edge of the southward sprawl of London, a few cottages remain amid modern housing, particularly in Leas Road, where some seventeenth-century almshouses survive.

At nearby Hamsey Green, Kings Wood provides an excellent area for the study of wildlife. Badgers abound, and there are numerous birds to be seen during pleasant walks.

In the locality: East Surrey Museum, page 91; churches at Caterham, page 67; Chelsham, page 68; Farleigh, page 70; and Tatsfield, page 74.

West Clandon
Clandon Park, page 76.

West Horsley
Church of St Mary, page 75.

Westhumble
Chapel Farm and Animal Trail, page 107; St Michael's Chapel, page 75; Westhumble Chapel, page 87.

Weybridge
During the twentieth century Weybridge has maintained strong links with the transport industry. The famous Brooklands racetrack was situated on the edge of the town, whilst today Weybridge is the home of British Aerospace.

The Wey bridge was in Bridge Road. It originated in the twelfth century as a footbridge, but the current structure is nineteenth-century in date. A later bridge, in Weybridge Road, can be seen from here. Between the bridges, boats can be hired for use on the canal.

Brooklands Museum, page 100; **Elmbridge Museum**, page 101; **St George's hillfort**, page 64.

In the locality: Chertsey Museum, page 92; Claremont House, page 76; Claremont Landscape Garden, page 77; Cobham Bus Museum, page 93; Cobham Mill, page 103; Painshill Park, page 83; churches at Cobham, page 69; Shepperton, page 73; Whiteley Village, page 75.

Whiteley Village
225 acres (90 hectares) of land, 2 miles (3 km) north-west of Cobham, were purchased in 1911 for the erection of a village for 'thrifty old people'. The money for the project, £1 million, was left for the purpose by William Whiteley of Whiteley's Stores, who died in 1907. A competition limited to six architects produced a design by Frank Atkinson.

In the centre of the village, which is formal and symmetrical, is a monument to Whiteley in a circle of turf. Building plots are arranged around this, and an outer octagonal road. There are four radial roads between the cottages, for use by traffic, and a network of turfed streets. The buildings are of a varied and attractive range of styles, making Whiteley a pleasant community with its own village hall and church.

Church of St Mark, page 75.

In the locality: Brooklands Museum, page 100; Cobham Bus Museum, page 93; Cobham Mill, page 103; Claremont House, page 76; Claremont Landscape Garden, page 77; Elmbridge Museum, page 101; Painshill Park, page 83.

Wimbledon
Lawn Tennis Museum, page 101; Wimbledon Common, page 60.

Windlesham
Church of St John the Baptist, page 75.

Wisley

Royal Horticultural Society's Wisley Garden, page 85.

Witley

Church of All Saints, page 75; Witley Common, page 60.

Woking

Market days Monday to Saturday.

Until 1838 Woking was just a small village 2 miles (3 km) from the present town centre. This area is known as Old Woking. The district still preserves a few old cottages and large houses from the old market town, but little of thirteenth-century Woking Old Hall, a once favoured royal palace and birthplace of Mary Tudor in 1514.

The present town did not develop until the coming of the railway and the canal. Until the 1850s the area was open heathland. Then, a shortage of land for burials in London led to the founding of the London Necropolis Company, which acquired 2300 acres (905 hectares) of land at Brookwood for a cemetery. Only 400 acres (160 hectares) were used for burials, the coffins being transported from the capital by special trains. The rest of the land was sold for development and so Woking was born. A large part of the town reflects this Victorian origin, although the town centre has more recently been redeveloped into a mixture of modern shops and offices. There is a well-equipped leisure centre, cinemas and theatres.

In Oriental Road is the Shah Jehan Mosque. Founded in 1899 to cater for the needs of students attending the Oriental Institute in Maybury, it was the first mosque in Britain.

Church of St Peter, Old Woking, page 72; **Horsell Common**, page 53; **Horsell Common bell barrows**, page 64.

In the locality: Burpham Court Farm Park, page 107; Chobham Common, page 51; Newark Priory, page 82; Ripley Local History Museum, page 100; Royal Horticultural Society's Wisley Garden, page 85; churches at Bisley, page 66; Chobham, page 69; Ockham, page 72; Pyrford, page 73; and Worplesdon, page 75.

Wonersh

British Red Cross Museum and Archives, page 101.

Worplesdon

Church of St Mary, page 75; Whitmoor Common barrows, page 65.

Wotton

Church of St John, page 75; Deerleap Wood bell barrow, page 63.

The New Victoria Theatre at Woking, viewed across the Basingstoke Canal.

The Little Pond at Frensham.

Beech woodland at Box Hill.

3
The countryside

The Surrey Wildlife Trust (SWT) manages a range of nature reserves in the county, access to which is restricted for the benefit of wildlife. Details can be obtained from the SWT, Old School, School Lane, Pirbright, Woking GU24 0JN (telephone: 01483 797575).

Banstead Woods, Fames Rough and Park Downs (OS 187: TQ 274583). Car park at the junction of B2032 and B2219.

These are an extensive area of woods and chalk grassland on the fringes of Greater London. Banstead Wood is traversed by a dense network of footpaths and marked walks, enabling the visitor to explore this mixed woodland, which is home to many species of birds. Among these are woodpeckers, owls and goldcrests. The commoner woodland species such as blue tit, great tit and robin also occur. In summer they are joined by warblers, including chiffchaff, blackcap and wood warbler. Until the 1960s, the wryneck bred in the area, before its final disappearance from the south of England.

Fames Rough, on the south-eastern side of Banstead Wood, is an area of rough grassland, important for its flora. Part of the site is ploughed annually to encourage the rare cut-leaved germander.

Park Downs is a section of chalk grassland across the road from Banstead Woods, partly covered by scrub. The grassland is important for its chalk flora, whilst the hawthorn and other bushes form nesting sites for many birds. Several members of the warbler family breed at Park Downs, where volunteers work to keep a balance between grass and bushes.

Basingstoke Canal. Basingstoke Canal Centre, Mytchett Place Road, Mytchett GU16 6DD. Telephone: 01252 370073.
Centre open daily, except Mondays.

The Basingstoke Canal, begun in 1788, was completed in 1794, linking London and Basingstoke. It left the seventeenth-century Wey Navigation midway between New Haw and Byfleet, running westwards through Woking and past Pirbright Camp. At Frimley Green it turned south to enter Hampshire at Aldershot. Along the Surrey stretch it rose 185 feet (58.4 metres), using twenty-four locks. In Hampshire there was only a single lock in the remaining 21 miles (34 km) to Basingstoke. The canal was the first of the agricultural canals, taking farm produce to the capital and bringing fuel and other materials back. Trade reached a peak in 1838, after which a decline set in, under competition from the railways. There was a revival in the 1920s, but the canal had suffered financial difficulties from its earliest days. When part of the long Greywell Tunnel at the Basingstoke end collapsed in 1932, the canal was abandoned. Hampshire and Surrey county councils bought their respective sections in 1973 and 1976 and began a massive restoration programme with the aid of volunteers and unemployed people. The canal is now navigable again as far as the Greywell Tunnel. The work has been accomplished without ruining the range of plants and animals which had colonised the canal, making it one of the most important water habitats in Britain. Much of the wildlife can be seen from the well-maintained towpath. For some while there was considerable debate about the possibility of restoring the Greywell Tunnel, but this is now known to be home to the largest colony of Natterer's bats in Britain and is also used by smaller numbers of other bats. It has been declared a Site of Special Scientific Interest and could not be restored without destroying this important colony.

The Basingstoke Canal Centre provides an introduction to the world of narrowboats, barges and locks. Inside there is a life-size reconstruction of a typical barge cabin and

The Basingstoke Canal near Frimley.

displays outlining the history of canals in general and Basingstoke Canal in particular. Much of the wall is given over to a large map, with pictures and notes on places of interest along the canal. At the far end of the building is a reconstruction of part of the Greywell Tunnel, complete with bat pictures and sounds. The centre includes a video room, shop and tea room. Barge trips start from outside.

Blackheath (OS 186: TQ 037462). Between Chilworth and Shamley Green.

Blackheath is a large area of heathland, birch and pine woodland. The grey sandy soils are well drained, allowing for comfortable walking at all times of the year.

The area of pinewood is frequented by flocks of birds such as coal tit and goldcrest. Although they are not regular visitors, this is a good place to look out for crossbills. Other small birds, including flocks of finches, may be seen flitting through the patches of birch, particularly in winter.

Where not invaded by trees, Blackheath contains some fine stands of heather, attrac-

tive in its own right, especially when in flower, during the autumn. In this area the nightjar breeds, and tree pipit and yellowhammer may be seen or heard.

Bookham Commons (OS 187: TQ 122567).

These three commons, Great Bookham, Little Bookham and Banks Common, are owned by the National Trust. Except for some areas of gravel and alluvium, the soil is London Clay and consequently is frequently waterlogged in winter. Past grazing by commoners' animals kept down the blackthorn and hawthorn scrub, which is now invading.

The 447 acres (179 hectares) of the three commons have been surveyed by the London Natural History Society since 1941, the longest continuous study of its kind in Britain. About five hundred species of flowering plants have been found so far, as well as a wide variety of ferns, mosses, lichens and fungi.

In the open areas, vetches, tares and vetchlings grow amid the rushes and grasses. The patches of scrub, which are controlled, provide nesting sites for small birds such as warblers. Streams and marshy areas thread their way through these habitats. They are lined by water plants such as mint, water figwort, gipsywort and bur marigold. The climax vegetation of the commons is pedunculate oak, which is well represented.

As well as the birds, which include woodpeckers, tawny owls and woodcock, there are many other animals to be seen by the visitor. Shrews, mice and voles are represented; rabbits and grey squirrels are common. Species present, but less frequently seen, include roe deer, weasel, stoat and grass snake.

Box Hill Country Park (OS 187: TQ 179513).

The National Trust has acquired over a long period about 1000 acres (400 hectares) of beautiful countryside at Box Hill, now a country park. The facilities include an information centre, shop, restaurant and toilets. A leaflet available from the information centre outlines some nature trails around the estate.

Box Hill was named after the box tree, a small evergreen which grows on the steep cliffs above the river Mole. The hill is a mixture of mature woodland and open chalk grassland, rich in orchids and butterflies. The spectacular views to the south over the Weald attract thousands of visitors annually. The grass is grazed each winter by a flock of sheep to keep the scrub at bay and conserve the orchids. Box Hill can be approached from the A24 via the Zig Zag Road, which climbs the hill like a Swiss mountain pass.

Chantries, Guildford (OS 186: TQ 023485).

With the North Downs Way passing along one side and the Pilgrims Way along the hilltop, Chantries has been on the line of a long-distance trackway for thousands of years. The wooded slopes also provide a pleasant walk from Guildford to St Martha's Church, above Chilworth.

Managed by Guildford Borough Council, Chantries is an area of mixed woodland frequented by small mammals, including grey squirrels and common shrews. Many of the trees are large and reaching maturity and some areas have been cleared and replanted, to ensure the survival of the wood for future generations.

Many of the paths through the wooded areas have been waymarked. From the hilltop, there are good views to the south, over Shalford, towards the high ground around Hindhead.

Chobham Common (OS 186: SU 973643).

1445 acres (578 hectares) of this extensive area of heathland were purchased from Lord Onslow by Surrey County Council in 1968, for use as a public open space. Since then part of the area has been designated a national nature reserve.

Chobham Common is used for a wide range of activities, in addition to walking and horse riding. Orienteering and the flying of model aircraft are popular, as is watching wildlife. Ten car parks and a network of tracks provide easy access to all parts of the area.

This part of Surrey lies on the infertile Bagshot Beds, giving rise to this extensive area of heather, pine and birch. The dry areas are dominated by ling, bell heather, common and lesser gorse. In the many wet areas there are cross-leaved heath, cotton grass, sphagnum and sundew.

Many species of butterflies, moths, spiders and dragonflies occur, including several which are rare. Among the birds are uncommon species such as nightjar and woodcock.

Crooksbury Hill and Common (OS 186: SU 884462). Between Elstead and The Sands.

Crooksbury Common comprises 204 acres (82 hectares) of open heathland, bracken-covered hillsides, birch, pine and chestnut woodland. The area is crossed by several footpaths and bridleways, whilst Crooksbury Hill is a public open space and excellent viewpoint. There are several earthworks on the common (see chapter 4).

Croydon open spaces

The London Borough of Croydon has a surprising amount of open space, much of which lies to the south of the town, away from the continuous sprawl of London. However, one open space to the north is well worth a visit. **South Norwood Lake** lies between the districts of Crystal Palace and South Norwood. It was constructed as a reservoir for an ill-fated canal project in the early nineteenth century and is one of the few surviving reminders of the scheme. Today it is used for sailing and fishing. There is a good collection of waterfowl, including wigeon, pochard and Chinese goose.

Near central Croydon are the extensive **Lloyd Park** and wooded **Addington Hills**. A little further south, **Croham Hurst** is a pleasant woodland area with grassy glades. **Selsdon Wood**, south-east of the town, is an important bird sanctuary, owned by the National Trust. Nearby **Kings Wood** was planted to a definite plan. Many archaeological remains have been found within its boundaries, and there have been quarries there in the past. Today it is well populated by badgers. Further south still, **Farthing Downs** and **Riddlesdown** are noted for their chalk flora, the former displaying a fine set of lynchets, banks formed between fields by ancient ploughing. Adjoining Farthing Downs are **Happy Valley Park** and **Devilsden Wood**, where yet more walks may be enjoyed.

Devil's Punchbowl, Hindhead (OS 186: SU 892358).

Just north of Hindhead is one of the most spectacular landscape features in the south of England. The A3 follows the rim of a deep valley known as the Devil's Punchbowl. The valley is mostly wooded, except for a few cottages and tiny farms at the bottom. A small stream flows close to the youth hostel.

Over the A3 are more extensive commonlands, very largely comprising open heather. Owned by the National Trust, they are a haven for wildlife. There are marked nature trails around the area, starting from a large car park at Hindhead.

Downs Link long-distance path

Opened in 1984, the Downs Link path mostly follows the track of a disused railway line from Guildford to Sussex. Starting from St Martha's Hill above Chilworth, it runs through the Wealden countryside to link the North Downs Way with the South Downs Way. Its origin as a railway track ensures that it is well drained and that there are no steep inclines.

Epsom Common (OS 187: TQ 184611).

A large common on the sticky London Clay, Epsom Common is a mixture of grassland and scrubby woodland. Near Malden Rushett there are two ponds. The one nearest the car park is much used by local fishermen. The other lake, covering almost 6 acres (2.4 hectares), was recreated by volunteers in 1976, having been dry for many years. Both lakes were once stew ponds, used by the monks of Chertsey Abbey to rear fish for stews. The ponds now attract a variety of wildfowl, including little grebe and mandarin duck.

Frensham Country Park (OS 186: SU 846407).

Frensham Country Park comprises an extensive area of heathland, together with a lake, to the south of Farnham. The heathland is dominated by ling and bell heather, with purple moor grass in the wetter areas. The heathers provide food and shelter for many snakes, lizards, small mammals and insects. A walk on a damp autumn morning will reveal the number of spiders present, when their webs glisten in the sunlight. Parts of the country park suffer from an invasion of silver birch and pine which is being controlled.

The Great Pond was created in the thirteenth century by monks from Winchester for rearing fish. Many species of birds, such as reed bunting, nest in the reed beds surrounding the lake. These are also the haunt of several species of dragonfly. Fishing is let to the local angling club. Frensham Sailing Club also uses the pond.

There is a wide network of footpaths, providing access to all parts of the country park, and 10 miles (16 km) of bridleways. A car park near the Great Pond is convenient for all facilities.

Greensand Way long-distance path

The Greensand Way long-distance footpath was opened on 15th June 1980. The route is 55 miles (88 km) long, beginning at Haslemere and running to the Kent border near Westerham.

The route follows the Lower Greensand hills, which cross the county from east to west, south of the North Downs. The path passes around the spectacular Devil's Punch-bowl and over Leith Hill, the highest point in south-east England.

Greensand is well drained and comfortable to walk on, making this a pleasant journey at any time of the year. The path passes through or near many towns and villages and is well served by public transport. The route is marked by the letters GW on footpath and bridleway signs. A guide book is available from Surrey County Council.

Hackhurst Local Nature Reserve, Gomshall (OS 187: TQ 094487).

Hackhurst Downs is an area of chalk grass-land and scrub owned by Surrey County Council and the National Trust. Work has been carried out to clear the invading hawthorn scrub from this reserve. As a result, a fine stand of juniper has been preserved. This plant was once much commoner across the county, as can be judged by the number of place-names incorporating the word 'juniper'. It is a slow-growing plant which cannot compete with haw-thorn. Another interesting species found here is the beautiful round-headed rampion.

The reserve is a fine example of chalk downland. A wide range of flowering plants supports a diverse fauna of butterflies, moths and other insects. Particularly obvious are the mounds made by yellow meadow ants. These mounds are used as lookout posts by rabbits and provide food for green woodpeckers, which eat the ants.

Headley Heath (OS 187: TQ 204539).

Situated on a sandy outcrop high on the North Downs, Headley Heath is a favoured place for walking and horse riding. Bracken covers large parts of the heath, but heather has been re-established in many areas. On the acidic soils, some birch woods have devel-oped. These support a wide selection of fungi in autumn. Behind Box Hill village there are some dry chalk valleys, which are alive with rabbits. Roe deer can be seen here, and night-ingales heard on a summer evening.

Horsell Common (OS 186: TQ 014604).

In 1898, when *The War of the Worlds* was published, Horsell Common found fame as the place where the Martians landed. The large sand pits where H. G. Wells set part of his story can still be seen.

Horsell Common is an area much divided by roads, but very diverse in habitat. There are patches of woodland, heath and grass, as well as streams and boggy areas. This diver-sity makes it an excellent area for studying wildlife. Birds from finches and tits to crows and kestrels may be seen. The grassland areas on the edge of the common are good places to see winter visitors such as fieldfare and redwing, as well as coveys of partridges. The varied plant life provides for a large number of insect species, whilst in autumn the com-mon is a good place to study fungi.

Horton Country Park, Epsom (OS 187: TQ 190625).

Horton was the name of a long-vanished medieval settlement, positioned between Ep-som and Ewell. By the nineteenth century Horton Place was a large country estate. This was bought by London County Council around 1900 to develop a series of mental hospitals. Each hospital had its own farm. Horton Country Park owes its foundation to the purchase by the Borough Council in 1973 of two farms surplus to requirements.

The country park enjoys a rolling agricul-tural landscape interspersed with blocks of woodland. An area of about 50 acres (20 hectares) is devoted to haymaking. Before the hay is cut, wild flowers may be enjoyed by visitors, as no herbicides are used in the meadows.

The woodlands are full of flowers in early spring. Throughout the year they are home to many species of birds including woodpeckers and treecreepers. In the summer chiffchaff, blackcap and other birds may be seen.

The park is crossed by an excellent net-work of footpaths and includes an equestrian centre, polo club, car parks and visitor centre. There are also a working farm with rare breeds, craft shops, tea room, gift shop and adventure playground.

Hurtwood Control (OS 187: TQ 098433).

Hurtwood Control is a voluntary organisa-tion concerned with the administration of

Leith Hill Tower is on the highest point in south-east England.

some 4000 acres (1600 hectares) of privately owned forest between Holmbury St Mary and Chilworth. To this area the public have been granted access 'for air and exercise'. The land includes Holmbury Hill, Hurtwood, Pitch Hill, Reynards Hill, Winterfold, Farley Heath, Shere Heath and parts of Blackheath and Smithwood Common.

It is largely commercial forest, engaged particularly in the growing of Scots pine. There is an extensive network of footpaths and firebreaks, but few waymarks. As the region is isolated, a map and compass are advisable. Twelve numbered car parks have been provided for visitors.

The Hurtwood area is rich in wildlife, especially roe deer, which may be frequently seen. It includes an iron age hillfort at Holmbury Hill (page 64) and the site of a Romano-British temple at Farley Heath (page 63). Many of the roads crossing the area are narrow and deeply cut into the sandstone.

Leith Hill (OS 187: TQ 131433).

5 miles (8 km) south of Dorking, Leith Hill is the highest point on the Greensand ridge and, at 967 feet (294 metres), the highest point in south-east England. It is topped by a tower, bringing its total height to 1000 feet (305 metres). On a clear day there are excellent views south, over the Weald, to the Channel coast, as well as north to London and the Chilterns. The tower, which was built in 1766 by Richard Hull, has been converted into an information centre and tea room by the National Trust. Much of the land at and around Leith Hill is owned by the National Trust. Mostly it is heath and woodland, with vast quantities of bilberry, heather and pine

Leith Hill Woods, a wild rhododendron garden owned by the National Trust on the slopes of Leith Hill, was almost destroyed by the 1987 storms. Restoration will be a very long process.

Lightwater Country Park, near Camberley (OS 186: SU 916619).

Lightwater Country Park is part of Bagshot Heath. 143 acres (57 hectares) were designated as a country park in 1973. They comprise largely heathland, with areas of pine and birch and some open water. Within the park are two marked walks and a nature trail, a visitor centre devoted to the heathland habitat and a sports centre.

Patient visitors may well see both pipistrelle bats and roe deer, especially towards the evening. Reptiles include the common lizard, grass snake and adder. Over eighty species of birds frequent the area, including more unusual ones such as redpoll, siskin and stonechat. Breeding in the small water areas are various species of dragonfly, which hover around the park. On hot days the grasslands are alive with the singing of grasshoppers. In addition to these habitats, there is an area of acid bog. This has a range of sphagnum mosses, bog asphodel, cotton grass and the insectivorous sundew.

Limpsfield Chart and Common (OS 187: TQ 427523).

In south-east Surrey, on the oldest rocks to reach the surface in the county, are Limpsfield Chart and Common. Surrounded by stone cottages, this extensive tract of countryside is owned by the Forestry Commission and the National Trust.

Mostly mixed woodland and heathland, the area is very attractive, with some fine beech trees. Parts are also planted with conifers, but there are frequent sunny glades and broad tracks, frequented by butterflies. There are several parking areas and places where a picnic may be enjoyed.

Morden Hall Park, Morden Hall Road, Morden SM4 5JD (OS 176: TQ 262687). Telephone: 0181-648 1845.

This National Trust property comprises 124 acres (50 hectares) of the parkland surrounding Morden Hall, providing an oasis of green in south-west London. Once an historic deer park, the area now includes the banks of the river Wandle, mature trees, woodland, grassland and fen. There is a shop, café, visitor facilities, garden centre and riverside walks, all just a short walk from Morden underground station. The old snuff mill is now an environmental education centre. There is a good range of wild flowers,

butterflies, dragonflies and birds.

Newlands Corner (OS 186: TQ 042495). On the A25 near Guildford.

Served by a large car park, Newlands Corner is a favoured place for a country picnics. As well as a large area of woodland and hawthorn scrub, there are acres of open, breezy, chalk grassland, which in summer is covered in wild flowers including orchids, rock-rose, field scabious and marjoram.

From the car park there are footpaths to Albury, Chilworth, Guildford and West Clandon. In addition, the North Downs Way climbs the hillside on its way from Farnham to Dover. There are good views from the top, which, at around 500 feet (152 metres) above sea level, overlooks the ancient Weston Wood, as well as Blackheath.

Norbury Park (OS 187: TQ 158535).

An important landscape feature in the Mole valley, Norbury Park is an open space owned by Surrey County Council. Much of the valley bottom is farmland, through which flows the meandering river Mole. Many species of water plants can be found growing here. The occasional heron or kingfisher visits this stretch of river.

On the hills above the river grow attractive beech and yew woods. The Druids Grove, a line of old yew trees, is worth a visit.

North Downs Way long-distance path

Opened in 1978, the North Downs Way runs 141 miles (226 km) from Farnham in Surrey to the Channel coast at Dover. In Surrey the route is marked by oak fingerpoints and stencilled acorn marks on gateposts.

Starting near Farnham station, the route soon passes through meadows alongside the river Wey. It then continues through the villages of Seale and Puttenham, to the south of the Downs, past the Watts Gallery, Compton (see page 93), and into Guildford.

The first steep climb comes after passing through Chantries, a wooded hill to the east of Guildford. The top of the next hill is crowned by St Martha's Church (see page 68) in an isolated setting. After descending from this Greensand hill, the route climbs again to cross the breezy slopes of Albury Downs, reaching the A25 at Newlands Corner.

The North Downs Way now becomes a wide track through woodland, along the crest of the Downs, as far as the Mole Gap. After crossing the A24, the river Mole is negotiated by stepping stones, before the steep ascent to Box Hill. Between here and Colley Hill, the path descends through Betchworth Quarry, where there are some interesting industrial monuments (see page 102).

After Reigate there is an attractive parkland section at Gatton, before the M25 is crossed at Merstham. A short distance later the M23 is also crossed. This is followed by a walk along the hilltop, before passing through woodland to the south of Caterham. From here, there are several more miles of hilltop walking, before reaching the Kent border near Westerham.

There is no need for the North Downs Way to be tackled as a continuous walk. The route passes through or near several towns, namely Farnham, Guildford, Dorking, Reigate and Oxted, where there are regular rail services. There are connecting bus services between these towns, although some are irregular, especially at weekends. It is a relatively easy route to walk, with only occasional steep sections, most of which have been provided with steps.

Nower Wood, near Leatherhead (OS 187: TQ 194546). Telephone: 01372 379509.
Open to the public on the third Sunday in each month from April until October.

81 acre (32 hectare) Nower Wood occupies a prominent position at the head of the Little Switzerland Valley, near Leatherhead. This mixed woodland with four ponds is a nature reserve and environmental education centre, run by the Surrey Wildlife Trust. Apart from usual woodland flora and fauna, Nower Wood is noted for its mass of bluebells each spring. A large number of roe deer live in the reserve and adders are usually visible during the summer, basking in the sun.

Puttenham Common (OS 186: SU 919461).

South of the Hog's Back, the 470 acres (188 hectares) of Puttenham Common are managed by Surrey County Council as a public open space. The main part of the common is an attractive area of sandy heathland dominated by ling, purple moor grass and sheep's fescue. This slopes down to a chain of lakes, set in a deep valley to the west. The rest of the area is woodland, with some damp alder scrub.

In addition to a network of footpaths and bridleways, Puttenham Common is crossed by the North Downs Way. The common is served by three car parks, with excellent views from the most easterly one.

Anglers on the tarn at Puttenham Common.

Riders in the sunshine at Richmond Park.

Ranmore Common (OS 187: TQ 142503).

On the slopes above Dorking, Ranmore Common comprises nearly 500 acres (200 hectares) of woodland, owned by the National Trust. In addition, there are 245 acres (98 hectares) of land on the southern slopes of the North Downs, parts of which are grazed by sheep in winter. This prevents encroachment of scrub, thus maintaining a habitat for orchids. Much of the woodland is a mixture of broad-leaved species growing on clay-with-flints, a geological deposit found on top of the Downs.

A wide variety of woodland birds inhabit this area, whilst further to the west goldcrests frequent the coniferous plantations managed by the Forestry Commission. From the western car park a forest trail has been laid out. There are several small ponds scattered across the common, and a few cottages of flint. Deep in the woods is Tanners Hatch Youth Hostel, amazingly isolated for a county like Surrey.

Richmond Park (OS 176: TQ 200730).

Richmond Park, at 2470 acres (1000 hectares), is the largest of London's royal parks. It was first enclosed in 1637 by Charles I as a hunting park, yet it was not until the time of William III and his wife Mary that the public were allowed access.

The best-known feature of Richmond Park is its herds of fallow and red deer. About six hundred deer roam the woods and open spaces. These are not the only mammals present. Foxes and grey squirrels are common. Several badger setts exist, as do small populations of weasel, stoat and hedgehog. Mice, shrews, rabbits and probably three species of bat may also be seen by the patient observer.

About one hundred species of birds have been recorded, taking advantage of the range of habitats. In the north-western part of the park, Sidmouth Wood is closed to the public because it is a bird sanctuary. On the Pen Ponds, in the centre of the park, the splendid great crested grebe nests, along with pochard, coot, moorhen, mallard, tufted duck, mute swan and Canada goose. The open woodland atmosphere encourages jackdaw, starling, tree sparrow, little owl, kestrel and redstart.

Between Kingston Gate and Pen Ponds is the Isabella Plantation. This 42 acre (17 hectare) plantation has been developed as a

The countryside

colourful woodland garden since planting commenced in 1951. With two streams running through it, this area of rhododendrons, azaleas, camellias, magnolias and heathers is a delight to visit from spring until autumn.

There are nine car parks and several miles of road and track through Richmond Park, open during the day. Refreshments are available from two restaurants. Several lodges are scattered around the park. Thatched House Lodge, closed to the public, is the home of Princess Alexandra.

Rowhill Copse, Weybourne (OS 186: SU 854497).

On the Surrey/Hampshire border near Aldershot, Rowhill Copse covers 52 acres (21 hectares). It serves as an open space for the town and is owned by Rushmoor Borough Council. There is a wide range of plants and trees as well as a host of freshwater life on the reserve.

There are two ponds in Rowhill Copse, which were once clay and sand pits. These support a community of fish and plants and provide a nesting site for water birds. In the north-west of the wood is a series of springs which form the source of the river Blackwater. In the centre of the wood, a $4^1/2$ acre (2 hectare) grassy clearing forms an attractive feature.

In 1968 the Rowhill Nature Reserve Society was formed. It has set up a field centre in the copse, which is used by schoolchildren for nature study.

Silent Pool, Shere (OS 187: TQ 061486).

This small open space comprises an attractive pool surrounded by woodland, close to the A25, and owned by Surrey County Council. It is fed by a chalk spring and linked in legend with King John. It is at the centre of a good footpath network and there is easy access to the North Downs Way and Newlands Corner. The pretty village of Shere is nearby.

South Park Farm, Blechingley (OS 187: TQ 342488).

South Park Farm is largely on the sticky Weald Clay, near its junction with the Lower Greensand. It is primarily a dairy farm and covers 1300 acres (522 hectares). By the

house, in the chapel of St Mark, a small information centre has been set up, depicting the natural history of the area. Guides to two farm nature trails can be purchased from here.

The farm is approached down a steep hill, running south from an unclassified road across Tilburstow Hill, at map reference TQ 344501.

Staffhurst Wood (OS 187: TQ 410486). Midway between Oxted (Surrey) and Edenbridge (Kent).

Staffhurst Wood is a local nature reserve managed by Surrey County Council. The wood has also been designated a Site of Special Scientific Interest, as it is one of the few remaining areas of ancient Wealden woodland.

Staffhurst Wood is a tract of mixed oak woodland, managed on the coppice with standards system. A limited number of selected trees were allowed to grow to maturity. These provided a light canopy over the coppiced areas, which were cut down to the stump every few years. The shoots then grew again until they reached the required size for crafts such as hurdlemaking. In Staffhurst Wood hornbeam, beech and ash were coppiced and oak left as standard trees.

Other trees and shrubs to be found in the wood include sycamore, birch, field maple, wild service tree, holly, yew and hazel. A visit is particularly recommended in spring, when there is a mass of bluebells.

Staines Reservoir and Moor (OS 176: TQ 050730 and TQ 035730).

North of Staines town centre is one of the most accessible of the Thames valley reservoirs. Crossed by a public footpath, it is one of the most important sites in Britain for water birds, especially in winter. Various species of gull, tern, grebe and duck may be seen, including smew.

Adjoining the King George VI Reservoir is Staines Moor, a rare survival in this region. It is an area of grassland on the alluvial gravels, threaded by streams and ditches. It has long been scheduled as a Site of Special Scientific Interest but is constantly under threat from companies wishing to extract the gravel which lies beneath. In winter flocks of golden plover congregate here.

The Thames Path

The Thames Path, a long-distance trail devised by the Countryside Commission, closely follows the river for 213 miles (340 km) from the river's source, near Kemble in Gloucestershire, to the Thames Barrier at Greenwich. It is unique in being the only long- distance path to follow a river and pass through major towns and cities. The path enters Surrey at historic Runnymede and continues through Staines to Chertsey and Walton-on-Thames. Skirting Bushy Park and Hampton Court Park it continues through Kingston and Richmond before passing Kew Gardens and heading for central London.

Thursley Common (OS 186: SU 900416).

A National Nature Reserve, this extensive common is a haven for the numerous insects which depend on heather. It is also one of the most easterly sites in Britain where the rare Dartford warbler may be found. Among the unusual birds of prey seen on the common are hobby and harriers.

Thursley also has one of the most extensive bogs in this part of England, providing a home for insectivorous plants such as sundews. These plants absorb nutrients from the insects they capture, to supplement the meagre quantities found in the poor soil. Many species of dragonfly breed in the bog pools, making Thursley one of Europe's most important areas for these insects.

Vann Lake (OS 187: TQ 156395).

Vann Lake is an old hammer pond set in a steep-sided wooded valley between Capel and Ockley. The lake covers 8 acres (3.2 hectares) and was created in the eighteenth century by damming a stream which flows down from the Lower Greensand. This goes on to become the Sussex river Arun.

The lake is surrounded by mixed deciduous woodland, including unusual trees such as the wild service tree. More than five hundred species of fungi have been recorded in the woods, which are also home to birds such as the nightingale.

The lake and woodlands are a nature reserve of the Surrey Wildlife Trust and can be viewed at all times from a waymarked path. The reserve can be reached by public footpaths from Ockley village green. To make special parking arrangements nearer the site or to obtain a copy of the nature trail guide, contact Surrey Wildlife Trust (telephone: 01483 488055).

Virginia Water (OS 176: SU 979687).

The Surrey/Berkshire border passes through the middle of this enormous lake on the edge of Windsor Great Park. A well-known beauty spot, the lake was constructed in 1746 by the Duke of Cumberland, third son of George II and commander of the British army at Culloden. There are several follies and 'ruins' around the edge, and a genuine totem pole from British Columbia, Canada. A large number of water birds may be seen at Virginia Water, among the most beautiful of which are mandarin duck.

The totem pole at Virginia Water.

Wallis Wood (OS 187: TQ 122389).

These 32½ acres (13 hectares) of oak and hazel coppice woodland a short walk from Walliswood village are owned by the Surrey Wildlife Trust. The trees are a mix of oak, ash, hornbeam, midland hawthorn, wild apple, wild cherry and wild service. Coppicing has led to the development of a ground flora of bluebells, broad-leaved helleborines, primroses, wild daffodils, wood-sorrel and many others. All this provides an excellent habitat for woodland birds and insects. Visitors are welcome but dogs must be kept on a lead. A leaflet is available from Surrey Wildlife Trust (telephone: 01483 488055).

Wey Navigation Canal

Opened to traffic in 1653 as far as Guildford, the Wey Navigation is still in constant use, although mainly by pleasure craft. It was extended to Godalming in 1763. The entire length is under the care of the National Trust. Sir Richard Weston, who lived at Sutton Place, was responsible for its construction. Along the route, many pieces of the original canal machinery and buildings remain. Walks along the towpath are popular, especially the section between Byfleet and Send.

Wimbledon Common (OS 176: TQ 231724).

It was only in 1871 that Wimbledon Common was acquired for public use. Since that time many trees have been planted and, in the more open parts, have invaded. The grassland is dominated by purple moor grass, with ling in some places. Many alien plants may be found, most likely introduced in garden rubbish from the surrounding district. The woodlands are mostly oak and birch. There are many other species here too, and the woods are good places to look for fungi in the autumn. Bogs and pools provide a habitat for interesting plants like marsh pennywort,

bur marigold and lesser spearwort. Many butterflies, including small tortoise-shell and peacock, are abundant. Fox and badger are the most interesting mammals to be seen.

Witley Common (OS 186: SU 934407). Information centre: Witley Common, Witley, Godalming GU8 5QA. Telephone: 01428 683207.

Information centre open April to October, Monday to Thursday. Common open at all times.

Owned by the National Trust since 1921, Witley Common is traversed by three nature trails. These start from the information centre and have been designed to draw attention to different aspects of the common: its natural history, management, and landscape and ecology. The centre itself includes an exhibition illustrating the wildlife and history of the common, and there is a ten-minute audio-visual display.

During two world wars, the commons were used as camps for British and later Canadian soldiers. Foreign soil from a sandpit at Seale, imported when the common was reinstated after the war, contained a significant amount of chalk, so that now, unusually, chalk plants grow in the centre of acid heathland. A large part of the common is woodland with a variety of species including oak, chestnut, silver birch, pine, willow and hawthorn. Without management, woodland would quickly take over the open areas too. Even more variety is ensured by a small acid bog, which is crossed on a boardwalk.

The range of habitats makes for a wide variety of species. In addition to the commoner birds like chaffinch, siskin, crossbill and woodlark may be noted. The commonest mammal is the rabbit, but foxes and roe deer are frequent too. Rarer sightings have included stoats and weasels. Adders, Britain's only poisonous snakes, are common but usually disappear well in advance of passers-by. In autumn several hundred species of fungi can be found.

4
Places of archaeological interest

Compared to surrounding counties, Surrey is rather poor in archaeological remains. During the half million years since the start of the palaeolithic, the area covered by the present county seems to have been unevenly settled.

Palaeolithic finds are mostly limited to large stone hand axes, which tend to turn up at random in the river gravels of the county. These were used to hunt animals, which supplemented a diet of whatever fruits could be collected. Palaeolithic material has come particularly from the river terraces of the Wey, near Farnham.

Mesolithic man (about 8000 to 4000 BC) seems to have preferred the sandy heathlands of western Surrey. The light woodland vegetation of such areas would have been particularly suitable for his food-gathering activities and nomadic way of life. Waste flakes have been found in quantities in several parts of the county, indicating old flint-working floors. Traces of associated occupation sites have been less frequent, but a pit dwelling is preserved in a shed at Abinger.

A more settled way of life developed during the neolithic period. This was marked by the use of hand-made pottery and the introduction of agriculture. Unlike other parts of Britain, there are no visible remains of this period in Surrey.

One of the commonest types of archaeological site to be seen in the county today is the bronze age burial mound. There are many in existence, although only a few are in good condition. Records of the contents of those which have been excavated are few, largely because of unscientific excavation in the nineteenth century. There have been excavations of occupation sites in places such as Weston Wood, Albury, but nothing visible remains. An important bronze age site was found at Runnymede Bridge, during construction of the M25. A trackway runs along the North Downs through Surrey on its way from the Channel coast to Salisbury Plain. This was an important communication route which seems to have remained in use at least until medieval times.

Two important types of iron age site have made their mark on the Surrey landscape. The most obvious of these are the hillforts, which are concentrated into two groups. The first group, along the Thames valley, has suffered to varying extents from development or its associated effects. The others are positioned along the Greensand ridge above the Weald. The precipitous slopes of these hills made their defences very effective.

The other feature of this period is the iron age, or Celtic, field system. The fields were roughly square in shape, as the light ploughs made cross-ploughing necessary. Where these fields were situated on slopes, soil moved downhill with each ploughing, forming banks across the hillsides. Examples of such field systems can be seen at Farthing Downs and on the slopes of Box Hill.

In AD 43 the Romans successfully invaded Britain. Despite its proximity to the point of invasion in Kent, Surrey seems to have played a less important role in Roman

Britain than some surrounding counties. Roman roads were constructed across the county, the best-known being Stane Street, which linked Chichester to London. Posting stations were positioned at regular intervals along these roads to serve as overnight stopping places. One was probably in the Ewell or Merton area, and another somewhere near Dorking. All these places have produced quantities of Roman pottery.

Villas, another well-known feature of Roman Britain, occur at sites across Surrey, but most were excavated in the nineteenth century, and so there are only scanty records and no visible remains.

In two places, urban areas developed during the period of Roman occupation. One was opposite the City of London at Southwark, where excavations have produced many finds. The other was smaller, situated near the bridge at Staines.

Other features of the Roman period are two temples, a tile factory at Ashtead and a major pottery industry around Farnham. The pottery production was centred on Alice Holt Forest, just over the border in Hampshire, where much evidence can still be found.

As with most parts of Britain, Saxon remains are very scarce. The evidence is almost exclusively confined to cemeteries. Three major cemeteries were grouped near the river Wandle at Croydon, Mitcham and Hackbridge. These probably date from as early as the fifth century. Other cemeteries, such as Hawks Hill (Leatherhead) and Guildown (Guildford), were later. Saxon work can be seen in several churches, details of which will be found in chapter 5.

In the following gazetteer the number of the Ordnance Survey 1:50,000 map on which the site may be found is given, followed by the National Grid reference.

Abinger pit dwelling, Abinger (OS 187: TQ 112458).

Dr L. S. B. Leakey, more famous for his work at Olduvai Gorge, excavated this mesolithic site in 1950. The pit, 10 feet (3.05 metres) by 14 feet (4.25 metres), was only 3 feet (0.9 metre) deep. It had a ledge along its deeper side, which may have been a kind of bench. Post-holes outside the pit indicate that a simple shelter of bracken or saplings may have covered the site. Burnt material and stones at the west end suggest a hearth. More than one thousand tiny flints, called microliths, were found in the pit.

Although it would appear too small for an efficient working area and too exposed for a sleeping place, it has to be assumed that it served one of these functions for mesolithic man, about eight thousand years ago.

The soil has been consolidated and the pit preserved. It is covered by a shed, which also contains a small museum of finds from the site. Permission to visit and a key can be obtained from the Manor House.

Anstiebury hillfort, Coldharbour (OS 187: TQ 153440).

This circular iron age hillfort of about 11 acres (4 hectares) is sited about 800 feet (244 metres) above sea level on the Greensand hills. Except where the land drops steeply to the south and west, it is surrounded by two banks and ditches and a counterscarp bank. The two outer ramparts are less than 3 feet (1 metre) high, but the strongly revetted inner one is 6 feet (1.8 metres) high. Excavations by Hugh Thompson suggest construction in the second half of the first century BC. It is believed to have been reoccupied in mid first century AD. The entrance was on the east side. The hillfort is now covered with trees.

Ashtead Roman villa and tile works (OS 187: TQ 177597). See page 11.

Crooksbury Common, Elstead (OS 186: SU 893450).

Surrounded by a single ditch and bank are what archaeologists believe to be three bronze

The site of the Romano-British temple at Farley Heath.

age bell barrows. They vary in height from 6 to 9 feet (2 to 3 metres), and in diameter between 30 and 60 feet (9 and 18 metres). Their irregular spacing has led to suggestions that they may be bowl barrows, the ditch and bank being constructed at a later date. No knowledge of any contents exists.

Deerleap Wood bell barrow, Wotton (OS 187: TQ 118480).

This very overgrown barrow is 7 feet (2.1 metres) high and about 72 feet (22 metres) in diameter. There is a 21 feet (6.4 metres) wide berm, separating the mound from its surrounding ditch. An excavation took place in 1960 during which no burial was found. The mound was found to be of rubble, covering a central turf core. A bronze age date is suggested, but no conclusive proof has been obtained.

Farley Heath Romano-British temple (OS 187: TQ 052449).

Only some concrete setts and a brief plaque now mark the site of a Romano-British temple. A road led to Stane Street from this temple, which at 400 feet (121 metres) above sea level must have been visible for some distance.

Frensham Common bowl barrows (OS 186: SU 854407).

This group of four bronze age bowl barrows is conspicuously situated on a hilltop between the Great and Little Ponds. The group is arranged in a linear fashion. The southernmost barrow shows signs of past excavation, but no records remain.

Galley Hills barrows (OS 187: TQ 250607).

One of this group of four burial mounds was excavated in 1972, disproving the theory that they were of bronze age origin. The contents were found to be the remains of a wealthy Saxon warrior, buried with full military regalia. The barrow was later the site of a gallows, which was the cause of much disturbance to its fabric.

Hascombe hillfort (OS 186: TQ 004386).

This iron age hillfort is approached by footpath from Hascombe village. The path continues around three sides of the fort, where it occupies the single ditch. The very steep hillsides have, in addition, been artificially scarped, making them almost impregnable. On the north-east side, where the land does not drop away, there is a strong line of rampart and ditch. These earthworks turn outwards at right angles to form a 73 foot (22 metre) entrance passage. Finds from the 1931 excavations are in Guildford Museum.

Holmbury hillfort (OS 187: TQ 105430).

On the edge of a precipitous promontory, 857 feet (259 metres) above sea level, this hillfort is in a bad state of preservation. There were two ramparts and ditches defending the north and west sides but these are now difficult to trace because of old sand and gravel diggings. Excavations have shown the hillfort to have been built towards the end of the iron age, by Belgic peoples. There are spectacular views to the south, over the Weald.

Horsell Common bell barrows (OS 187: TQ 014598 and TQ 016598).

These two bell barrows are situated on either side of the road from Horsell to Maybury. Both appear to have been excavated in the past, but no reports are available. The western one is 100 feet (30.5 metres) in diameter and surrounded by a berm, which has an outer diameter of 160 feet (48.7 metres). The eastern barrow is approximately two-thirds the size of the other. A bronze age date is indicated, possibly between 1600 and 1400 BC.

Kent/Surrey border cross-valley dyke (OS 187: TQ 433535).

Following the Kent/Surrey border for several hundred metres is a linear earthwork of substantial proportions, possibly dating to the Saxon period. Its exact purpose is uncertain, but it was probably constructed to delineate some kind of boundary. The easiest point from which to view the earthwork is where the A25 crosses into Kent, near Westerham.

Newlands Corner round barrow (OS 186: TQ 045492).

To judge by the hollow in its summit, this barrow has been dug into in the past, yet nothing is known of its contents. It is 55 feet (16.7 metres) across and about 3 feet (1 metre) high. Sited in woods, it is of bronze age origin.

Reigate Heath barrows (OS 187: TQ 238505).

The Reigate Heath round barrows form a bronze age cemetery. Seven may be seen on a ridge to the east of the windmill, running in a line roughly north to south. The barrows range in diameter from 24 feet (7.3 metres) to 100 feet (30.5 metres). The largest of the group was opened in 1809 and produced a cremation burial. A neighbouring barrow also produced evidence of a cremation, but two others yielded nothing.

St George's hillfort, Weybridge (OS 187: TQ 085618).

This iron age hillfort is in an incomplete state of preservation because suburban housing has been built over it. As a result the iron age ramparts spread through a series of gardens and open spaces. The fort is of irregular shape and 14 acres (5.7 hectares) in area. It occupies a commanding position overlooking old fords across the rivers Mole and Wey, which come close to each other here. The hillfort defences consisted of a single rampart, except in the north-west, where it is doubled. A semicircular enclosure on the north-east could have been a cattle pound added after the main construction was completed. Evidence indicates occupation during the third century BC and first century AD.

Soldiers' Ring earthwork, Crooksbury Common (OS 186; SU 880462).

Just over 1 mile (1.6 km) north-west of some bronze age barrows lies this small circular enclosure. Its boundaries are formed by a single bank and ditch. The earthwork is believed to be an iron age animal enclosure.

Stane Street (OS 187).

The Roman road from London to Chichester has been known as Stane Street for at least seven hundred years. There have been various excavations along its length, which date it to the first century AD.

In Surrey none of the road surface is visible, but extensive sections are used by public footpaths and roads. In the north of the county it is possible to walk from Thirty Acre Barn (TQ 195569) to Juniper Hall (TQ 172530). Around Ockley, the route is used by the A29 for over 2 miles (3.2 km).

Sunningdale bowl barrow (OS 176: SU 952665).

Situated in a garden west of Ridge Mount Road is this bowl barrow 5 feet (1.5 metres) high and 71 feet (21.5 metres) in diameter. It can be seen from the road but there is no public access to it. A trench cut through it in 1901 revealed twenty-five cremation burials. Twenty-three of these were in bucket-shaped or barrel-shaped urns of a type known as Deverel-Rimbury. The burials were near the surface and so must be suspected to be later than the construction of the mound. The urns date to about 1200 BC. The barrow is believed to have been constructed in the bronze age around 1800 BC.

Whitmoor Common barrows, Worplesdon (OS 186: SU 997537).

In a wood on the edge of the common is this small bronze age bell barrow excavated by Pitt-Rivers. He found a small hole at the centre, 'where no doubt a burnt body had been deposited'. Close by were two bucket-type cinerary urns.

At SU 987534, on the south side of the common, is an even smaller barrow, also dug by Pitt-Rivers. This contained three bucket urns with burnt bones.

5
Churches and chapels

Any church or chapel in Surrey is worth a visit. Those listed here are some of the more interesting ones. The visitor may find some churches locked, particularly those near London. In such cases there is usually a notice displayed outside, giving details of local keyholders.

Abinger: St James. (South of A25, south-west of Dorking.)

This Norman church was badly damaged by a flying bomb during the Second World War and so needed extensive restoration. Further work was done in 1964, following a fire. The outside is attractive, but the interior is rather plain. There is an abstract stained glass window of 1967, by Lawrence Lee.

Addington: St Mary. (On A2022, south-east of Croydon.)

The burial place of five Archbishops, the church has a Norman chancel and windows, a thirteenth-century south arcade and some unusual memorials. There are church tours on the second and fourth Sunday afternoons in each month.

Albury Park: St Peter and St Paul. (On A248, south-east of Guildford.)

Disused since 1842, this church has been vested in the Redundant Churches Fund since 1974. The north nave wall and base of the central tower are Saxon. The rest of the tower is Norman with a small Norman window. The ruined chancel is thirteenth-century. The walls of the transept were elaborately decorated in the nineteenth century by Pugin, to form a family mortuary chapel for Henry Drummond, then owner of the adjacent mansion (see page 76). A large medieval wall painting of St Christopher remains, opposite the north entrance. The tower is surmounted by an unusual seventeenth-century shingled cupola.

Alfold: St Nicholas. (On B2133, south of Cranleigh.)

The south arcade is late twelfth-century;

the north arcade and chancel are fourteenth-century. The shingled bell turret is supported internally by four massive timbers. Old floor tiles remain around the altar. A Horsham-stone roof sweeps down low over the aisles.

Ashtead: St Giles. (On A24, between Epsom and Leatherhead.)

This church is largely nineteenth-century, except for a sixteenth-century tower. Quantities of Roman tile are visible in the outer walls. Roman and later material has been found near the church, and a major Roman complex existed on the common.

Beddington: St Mary. (On A232, between Croydon and Sutton.)

The church stands in a surprisingly rural setting on the edge of Beddington Park. Nave arcades, piers, tower, porch and possibly the chancel are fourteenth-century. The nave roof, chancel arch and chancel roof all date from a Victorian restoration. The organ gallery, with its painted dado and floral ornament, is by William Morris. The church contains a Roman coffin decorated with shell motifs.

Betchworth: St Michael. (South of A25, between Reigate and Dorking.)

The majority of this building dates from either the thirteenth or the fourteenth century. The Norman tower was central until 1851, when it was found to be unsafe. It was rebuilt at the south end. The church is built largely of grey firestone, a local calcareous sandstone named from its heat-resistant properties.

Bisley: St John the Baptist. (On A322, north-west of Woking.)

The oldest parts of this church set in fields,

Chaldon church is famous for its ancient wall-painting.

away from the village, are thirteenth-century and built of carstone. The north aisle and chancel are nineteenth-century.

Blechingley: St Mary. (On A25, east of Redhill.)

This large impressive Perpendicular church has a massive Norman tower and a Norman window in the east end.

Burstow: St Bartholomew. (North of B2037, south-east of Horley.)

This secluded church has a tower completely of timber at the west end. A blocked twelfth-century window can be seen between the main windows in the north wall. John Flamsteed, the first Astronomer Royal, was rector here from 1684 to 1719.

Camberley: St Paul.

Situated in Crawley Hill, away from the town centre, this half-timbered cottage-like church was built in 1907. The airy interior is largely red brick, with a timber and tile roof.

Carshalton: All Saints. (On A232, just east of Sutton.)

This is a big Perpendicular church, mostly of 1893-1914, by A. W. and R. Blomfield, but with medieval origins. The south aisle of the present church was the nave of the medieval one.

Caterham: St Lawrence.

This small church dates from the Norman period. The interior has few fittings remaining, as the church has largely been replaced by St Mary's opposite. The roofs are a mixture of styles – crownpost, queenpost and wagon – and constructed of rough timbers. Some indistinct traces of wall paintings are visible.

Chaldon: St Peter and St Paul. (North of B2031, west of Caterham.)

This isolated small Norman church contains a rare wall-painting dating to about 1200, depicting a subject that combines the Ladder of Salvation and the Last Judgement. The bell is also thirteenth-century.

Providence Chapel, Charlwood.

Charlwood: Providence Chapel. (North-west of Crawley.)

Situated in an anonymous cul-de-sac to the north of the Horley road, this is a simple weatherboarded chapel dating to about 1800. It is fronted by a large veranda and is unlike anything else likely to be encountered in England. It has the appearance of having been transported from Kentucky.

Charlwood: St Nicholas. (North-west of Crawley.)

This Norman church, with parts dating from about 1080, contains a screen which is the only large piece of medieval woodwork in Surrey. A fine crownpost roof is visible, and several fourteenth-century wall paintings may be seen on the south wall of the nave.

Chelsham: St Leonard. (North of B269, near Warlingham.)

It is unfortunate that this flint building, in a beautiful setting on the North Downs, has been so heavily restored. Several old graveboards remain in the churchyard.

Chertsey: St Peter.

This church is largely built in an early nineteenth-century Gothick style, except for a medieval tower and fifteenth-century chancel arch. The outside of the chancel has been renewed.

Chiddingfold: St Mary the Virgin. (On A283, south of Godalming.)

Much has been lost due to heavy restoration in 1869, but there is thirteenth-century work in the chancel and north chapel. The west window of the south aisle is made from fragments of glass collected from medieval glassworking sites in the vicinity.

Chilworth: St Martha on the Hill. (On A248, south-east of Guildford.)

Isolated on a heather-clad hilltop above the village, the church was mostly rebuilt in the mid nineteenth century, in an impressive Norman style, using the old materials of the ruinous church.

Chobham: St Laurence. (On A319, north-west of Woking.)

Windows in the south aisle are fifteenth-century, as are the tower and west porch. Inside, the south aisle is twelfth-century. Both the nave and south aisle are covered by one roof, which sweeps to within 8 feet (2.7 metres) of the ground.

Cobham: St Andrew. (South of A3, south of Walton-on-Thames.)

The west and south doors are both Norman. This church underwent extensive restoration and enlargement four times during the Victorian era. In the churchyard are a massive mausoleum to Harvey Combe and a grave-stone to David Archibald, who allegedly died on 31st February 1880.

Compton: St Nicholas. (On B3000, south-west of Guildford.)

The plain unbuttressed tower is eleventh-century, as are parts of the walls. As there are no Norman features in the bell-tower, it might possibly be pre-Conquest. In the twelfth century a two-storeyed sanctuary with a vaulted chamber below and a separate chapel above, separated from the chancel by an early wooden Romanesque guard rail, was installed. This is the only example of its kind in England.

Coulsdon: St John the Evangelist. (On A23, between Purley and Redhill.)

Placed on the corner of the old village green, the church has thirteenth-century origins, visible in the chancel arch, the windows of the north and south aisles, and the arcading. The stone and flint tower is fifteenth-century.

Crowhurst: St George. (East of A22, south of Oxted.)

Positioned on a hilltop, this is a simple church of the twelfth and thirteenth centuries. A cast-iron memorial painting to Anne Forster in the chancel floor provides a reminder of the Wealden iron industry. There is an enormous hollow yew tree in the churchyard.

Croydon: St John the Baptist.

Dating from the fifteenth century, this is Surrey's largest parish church and is the burial place of six Archbishops of Canterbury.

Dorking: St Martin.

This fine well-proportioned Victorian church by Woodyer has one of the highest parish-church spires in England, which dominates the town. The interior is tall, with acutely pointed arches.

Dunsfold: St Mary and All Saints. (South of B2130, south-east of Godalming.)

This church is almost completely of around 1270, although there have been a few minor alterations since. There is a small area of wall-painting but it cannot be deciphered. The original brick herringbone floor remains inside. The church is very atmospheric,

Dunsfold church has some of the oldest pews in England.

complete with simple wooden pews of the thirteenth century. The windows are late Geometrical in style, dating from the late thirteenth or early fourteenth century.

Esher: St George.

This small stone sixteenth-century church, just off the High Street, is well-kept and largely unrestored.

Ewhurst: St Peter and St Paul. (On B2127, east of Cranleigh.)

Built of local stone, this cruciform church has much character. The nave is probably Norman, with an impressive twelfth-century southern doorway. Tower arches and transepts are thirteenth-century. This church was partly rebuilt after the tower collapsed in 1837.

Farleigh: St Mary. (East of B269, south-east of Croydon.)

In a surprisingly rural setting, only 4 miles (6 km) from central Croydon, can be found this simple Norman church with a shingled bell turret. Almost the entire building dates from before 1250.

Farnham: St Andrew.

This large, mainly fifteenth-century town church has been excessively restored both inside and out. Some late twelfth-century features remain, particularly in the chancel. It contains a collection of hatchments. By the porch is the tomb of William Cobbett.

Fetcham: St Mary. (North of A246, west of Leatherhead.)

The western quoins of the nave and the wall above the south arcade are believed to be pre-Conquest. Roman brick is used in the window dressings and walls. The rest of the church dates from the medieval period.

Frimley: St Peter. (South of M3, between Camberley and Farnborough.)

A Perpendicular church of 1825, St Peter's was designed by J. T. Parkinson, the architect of Bryanston Square and Montague Square in London.

Godalming: St Peter and St Paul.

This mainly medieval church contains some pre-Conquest features visible only from the ringers' chamber. Norman work remains in the tower, chancel and transepts. The huge lead spire is a rare feature in this part of England. The shafting of the lancet lights in the south chapel is of Sussex marble.

Great Bookham: St Nicholas. (On A246, west of Leatherhead.)

A weatherboarded west tower adorns this church, which has twelfth-century arcades. An inscription records that the chancel was constructed by John Rutherwyke, Abbot of Chertsey, in 1341. Two blocked Norman windows can be seen above the north arcade. The north aisle was restored in 1845, having previously been blocked.

Guildford: Cathedral of the Holy Spirit.

The new diocese of Guildford was formed in 1927 and an open competition was held in 1932 for designs for a new cathedral to be built at the summit of Stag Hill half a mile (800 metres) from the centre of Guildford. The winner was Edward Maufe and in 1936 the foundation stone was laid for the cathedral to be built to his plans. It was the first cathedral to be built on a new site in the south of England since the Reformation. When the choir was almost completed, the Second World War brought work to a halt until the 1950s and the building was at last consecrated in 1961. Built in hand-made bricks made locally (many of them bought and signed by individuals) and enhanced by Clipsham stone and by gilded statues placed high on the massive central tower to the west and the apse to the east, the cathedral is an impressive prospect above the town. Within it is lofty, light and soothing, with white plastered walls and piers, and tall, deep windows. Against the pale flowing Gothic of the architecture the furnishings, such as the rows of blue embroidered kneelers and the sanctuary carpet, provide touches of colour.

Guildford: Holy Trinity.

Except for minimal earlier work, Holy Trinity dates entirely from the mid eighteenth century, following the collapse of the tower in 1740. A solid red-brick church with a

At Hascombe church Victorian wall-paintings depict St Peter and other disciples netting fish.

battlemented tower, it stands in the High Street. There is good ironwork and joinery.

Guildford: St Mary.

St Mary's is Guildford's most ancient church. Although the exterior has been restored, the interior is still attractive. The central flint and chalk tower dates from the eleventh century. There is much Norman work; the aisles were widened in the thirteenth century.

Hascombe: St Peter. (On B2130, south-east of Godalming.)

This excellent Victorian church of 1864 is by Woodyer. The outside is of local stone. Inside, the building is tall and dark with beautiful stained glass windows. The chancel is elaborately decorated. The nave was painted later, in 1890.

Laleham: All Saints. (Between Staines and Chertsey.)

The exterior is largely brick, with a nineteenth-century appearance. The chapel is early Tudor, and the tower early Georgian. Inside there are Norman arcades. Matthew Arnold, the poet, is buried in the churchyard.

Leatherhead: St Mary and St Nicholas.

The interior is largely early thirteenth-century. It contains a leather chest dated 1663, and in the tower there is a modern curtain embroidered with scenes of old Leatherhead. The tower is markedly out of alignment with the rest of the building.

Lingfield: St Peter and St Paul. (On B2028, north of East Grinstead.)

This is the only large-scale church of the Perpendicular style in Surrey. The tower is fourteenth-century; the rest was rebuilt by Sir Reginald Cobham when he founded a college for secular chaplains here in 1431. The building contains the finest collection of brasses in Surrey.

Littleton: St Mary Magdalene. (North-east of Chertsey.)

Parts of the chancel and nave are thirteenth-century, built of ragstone and flint rubble. The impressive brick tower is sixteenth-century. The porch, also of brick, is eighteenth-century and has a very unusual appearance.

Lower Kingswood: Jesus Christ the Wisdom of God. (On A217, north of Reigate.)

Built in 1891, this church is notable for its contents. The wooden roof is attractively painted inside, and there is spectacular decoration around the altar. Much of the interior work is of different marbles. The church contains several Byzantine capitals and sculptures of the fifth and sixth centuries from Ephesus.

Merstham: St Katherine. (On A23, north of Redhill.)

The church dates from the thirteenth century and has a large tower. It is set in a flint-walled churchyard on the slopes of the Downs, to the north of the village and the M25.

Mickleham: St Michael. (Off A24 between Leatherhead and Dorking.)

This church is of flint with a massive tower and tiny spire. The chancel is noticeably out of alignment and some Norman work can be seen inside the building. The wooden graveboards in the churchyard are a special feature and there is a large collection of hatchments inside the church. These heraldic memorials were particularly common between the seventeenth and nineteenth centuries.

Newchapel: London Temple Visitors' Centre. (On A22, north-west of East Grinstead.)

From the A22 near Lingfield can be seen the London Temple of the Church of Jesus Christ of Latter-day Saints, otherwise known as the Mormon Church. The temple itself is open only to followers of that sect, but a visitors' centre has been built adjacent to it, where the beliefs of the Mormons are explained. The temple grounds are also open.

Newdigate: St Peter. (East of A24, south-east of Dorking.)

Although much restored, the church has a thirteenth-century chancel and fourteenth-century south aisle. The fifteenth-century timber tower is like that at Burstow.

Oakwoodhill (or Okewoodhill): St John the Baptist. (West of A29, north-west of Horsham.)

On a grassy knoll in a wood, far from the village, the church was built in the thirteenth century as a chapel of ease to Wotton. It was almost doubled in size in 1879 by the addition of a north aisle. Fragments of two thirteenth-century wall-paintings are visible on the south wall of the chancel. The kneelers, made by parishioners between 1974 and 1976, illustrate the history of the church.

Ockham: All Saints. (On B2039, north-east of Guildford.)

Isolated in a parkland setting, the most notable feature of this church is its seven-lancet thirteenth-century window. It has been suggested that this may have come from nearby Newark Priory following the Dissolution of the Monasteries.

Old Woking: St Peter. (South of Woking.)

The Norman north door of the nave remains, pierced by Perpendicular windows. The chancel and tower are fifteenth-century. Under the tower is a tall, carved west doorway, which appears to date from around 1100. It still has the original Romanesque door.

Outwood: St John the Baptist. (East of M23, south-east of Redhill.)

This plain church was built in 1869, with a simple brick interior. The impressive tower was added by Manning in 1876.

Oxted: St Mary.

This ironstone and rubble church has a squat tower and is set in a circular churchyard. Despite restoration, the interior retains an ancient atmosphere. The four stained-glass evangelists in the tracery lights of the east window are believed to be of the fourteenth century and are among the oldest pieces of stained glass in Surrey. The four aisle windows are by Morris & Company but date from after the death of William Morris.

Peper Harow: St Nicholas. (West of A3, west of Godalming.)

This Norman church was restored by Pugin in the mid nineteenth century. The south wall is Norman, as is the plain south doorway. Much of the remainder is now of the Early English and Decorated styles.

Petersham: St Peter. (South of Richmond.)

The chancel is late thirteenth-century. The tower and transepts were added early in the seventeenth century, following a rebuilding of most of the church in the sixteenth century. The nave and tower are of brick. This church escaped extensive Victorian restoration, retaining its 1740 box pews and galleries, and is approached along a path from the main road.

Puttenham: St John the Baptist. (South of A31, west of Guildford.)

The four-bay north arcade is mid twelfth-

St Mary's church, Oxted, has windows by Morris & Company.

century. The plinths of the pillars rise as though the floor once sloped. The chancel arch is about 1200 and the tower fifteenth-century. By the path from the churchyard gate is the village well, recently discovered and restored.

Pyrford: St Nicholas. (South-east of Woking.)

This unaltered Norman church stands on a hilltop above the ruined Newark Priory. The Norman north door is attractively carved. Inside, there are several remnants of wall-paintings dating from 1200. In 1967 an earlier painting was discovered beneath, probably of about 1140 in date. Other interior features are the rather low chancel arch and fifteenth-century pews. A pictorial history of the church is displayed in the Tudor porch.

Ranmore: St Barnabas. (North-west of Dorking.)

The octagonal spire of this hilltop church is a prominent local landmark. By Sir George Gilbert Scott, the church is a fine building of 1859, with much marble internally. The exterior is faced with cobbles.

Reigate: St Mary Magdalene.

The exterior is very plain. Inside, the tall arcades of about 1200 are still intact. The piers do not match but form a pleasant mix of round, hexagonal and quatrefoil styles. The stained glass is bright and attractive, especially that in the chancel.

Shepperton: St Nicholas. (North of Walton-on-Thames.)

In an attractive square, this church has a brick, battlemented west tower. The church is early seventeenth-century, of flint rubble. It has a wooden gallery of nineteenth-century date, lending a romantic air to the building.

Shere: St James. (On A25, east of Guildford.)

The shingled spire is supported by an early Norman tower. The nave and part of the south

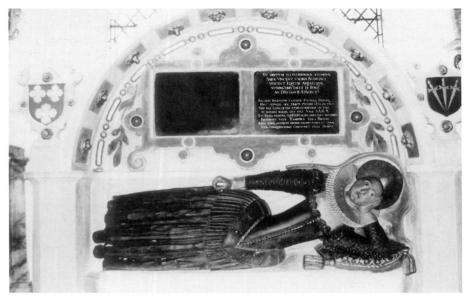

The monument to Lady Vincent in Stoke D'Abernon church.

transept walls are also Norman, as is the south door. In the chancel wall can be seen a quatrefoil and squint dating to the fourteenth century. Behind these was a tiny enclosed cell in which Christine Carpenter, an anchoress (or religious recluse), lived. Food was passed to her from the churchyard through a grid. The font dates to around 1200.

Stanwell: St Mary. (North of Staines.)

This church, at the end of a runway of Heathrow Airport, is tall and well-proportioned. The most interesting feature is the chequered tower of the thirteenth and fourteenth centuries. There is also a thirteenth-century south arcade and fifteenth-century roof. It stands in an attractive setting at the head of a small village green, despite surrounding suburbanisation.

Stoke D'Abernon: St Mary. (On A245, north-west of Leatherhead.)

Part of an apse inside the north chapel and a blocked doorway high in the south wall are said to be Anglo-Saxon. The doorway would

have led to a wooden gallery. The chancel is mid thirteenth-century and the Norbury Chapel late fifteenth-century. Quantities of reused Roman brick are visible in the walls, particularly on the south side. A good group of brasses includes one 6 feet 6 inches (1.95 metres) long of Sir John D'Abernon; it is late thirteenth-century and the oldest brass in England.

Tandridge: St Peter. (South of A25, southeast of Oxted.)

The main interest of this small church lies in its spectacular timberwork. The tower and shingled spire are supported by four massive oak corner posts with large cross braces. The roof is a mass of oak rafters said to date to 1300. A narrow slit window and doorway in the chancel are Norman, dating from around 1100. On the chancel arch is a twentieth-century wall painting and in the churchyard is one of the largest yew trees in Britain.

Tatsfield: St Mary. (West of A233, northeast of Oxted.)

The church is in a beautiful setting 790 feet

(241 metres) above sea level on the North Downs. The nave walls are totally Norman, with two Norman windows in the north side. The chancel is thirteenth-century. A copy of a Rubens painting of the Crucifixion hangs on the north wall.

Thorpe: St Mary. (North-west of Chertsey.)

The church has a seventeenth-century red-brick tower, thirteenth-century arcades, twelfth-century chancel arch and attractive mid nineteenth-century stained glass. Replicas of church brasses are available for rubbing in a modern church room.

Thursley: St Michael and All Angels. (West of A3, south-west of Godalming.)

Badly restored twice in the nineteenth century, this sandstone church with central belfry is approached by a deeply sunken path through the churchyard. There are two Saxon windows in the north wall of the chancel, and a Norman window above the north arcade. The fifteenth-century belfry is supported by an extraordinary timber cage in the centre of the nave. The font is possibly pre-Conquest.

Wanborough: St Bartholomew. (North of A31, west of Guildford.)

This tiny flint-built chapel was constructed in the thirteenth century. It was restored in 1862, having fallen into disuse in the seventeenth century. Apart from two windows in the Decorated and Perpendicular styles, all windows are thirteenth-century lancets.

West Horsley: St Mary. (On A246, north-east of Guildford.)

This is largely a thirteenth-century building, with fine circular piers forming the north arcade. A blocked half arch to the left of the chancel arch may have been for a rood stair. There is a group of early wall-paintings on the west wall, including a 13 feet (4 metres) high St Christopher. Stained glass includes a small window in the north side of the chancel, dated 1384.

Westhumble: St Michael's Chapel. (West of A24, north of Dorking.)

This old barn, dating to the seventeenth or eighteenth century, was converted into a chapel in 1901, following use as a place of rest for navvies building the neighbouring railway.

Whiteley Village: St Mark. (South of Walton-on-Thames.)

Built by Sir Walter Tupper in 1919 as part of a formal garden suburb, St Mark's is constructed in the Gothic style of 1300.

Windlesham: St John the Baptist. (South of A30, north-west of Camberley.)

Rebuilt in the seventeenth century using quoined brick, with later alterations, the church is in an attractive setting next to an eighteenth-century brick house, Cedars. It contains a chained copy of Bishop Jewel's *Apologie*.

Witley: All Saints. (On A283, south of Godalming.)

Remnants of the Saxon/Norman nave can be seen in the crossing tower. There are extensive traces of medieval wall-painting and a Norman doorway. It is a cruciform church on a knoll, in an attractive village.

Worplesdon: St Mary. (On A322, north-west of Guildford.)

The thirteenth-century north chapel has been badly restored. Also thirteenth-century are the arcades. The majority of the rest of the church is fifteenth-century. The cupola was transferred in 1766 from the rectory stables.

Wotton: St John. (On A25, west of Dorking.)

This Bargate-stone church stands, totally isolated, in an incomparable setting on a hilltop between the North Downs and the Greensand hills. The early Norman tower was central before the removal of the western part of the church in the thirteenth century. The foundations of this section still remain. John Evelyn, the diarist and silviculturalist, is buried here. His family home, Wotton House, is now a training college.

6

Historic buildings and gardens

Albury Park, Albury, Guildford GU5 9BB. Telephone: 01483 202964.
Open May to September, Wednesday and Thursday afternoons.

The original Tudor timber-framed house was largely rebuilt by John and George Evelyn during the seventeenth century. Changes were made about 1700, then by Soane in 1800 and again by Hakewill a short time later. In 1846-52 Augustus Welby Pugin altered the house, attempting to give it a Tudor appearance. In the course of his work he added sixty-three ornate chimneys of brick. The interior contains a plain staircase and drawing room by Soane. There is also an Adam fireplace and a seventeenth-century Dutch overmantel. The surrounding gardens were originally laid out by the Evelyns in the mid seventeenth century.

Carew Manor and Dovecote, Church Road, Beddington SM6 7NH. Telephone: 0181-773 4555.
Open April to October, Sunday and bank holiday Monday afternoons.

This building, used as a school during the week, was formerly known as Beddington Park or Beddington Place. Dating from the reign of Henry VIII, it also contains evidence of six-teenth- and eighteenth-century rebuilding. The Grade I listed late-medieval Great Hall is more than 60 feet (18 metres) long and 32 feet (9.75 metres) wide and preserves a fine hammerbeam and arch-braced roof. Guided tours are available, beginning at the unusual eighteenth-century octagonal dovecote, which still contains its original circular potence (ladder) to reach the 1200 nesting boxes.

Clandon Park, West Clandon, Guildford GU4 7RQ. Telephone: 01483 222482. National Trust.
Open April to October, daily except Thurs-

days and Fridays.

Built by Giacomo Leoni between 1713 and 1729 for the Onslow family, Clandon Park has been little altered since. It is a symmetrical red-brick house, with a white stone centrepiece, built in the Palladian style.

The house is entered through a vast two-storeyed hall. From this Marble Hall, the visitor passes to the Morning Room, containing a collection of family portraits and furniture dating to the eighteenth century. Through the Palladio Room, one reaches the Hunting Room, named after its extensive panels of Soho tapestry woven about 1740. The walls of the Green Drawing Room are lined with early eighteenth-century green wallpaper, printed on very small sheets. Several other rooms are open to the public, including the Blue Wallpaper Room, formerly the dressing room to the Prince Regent's Room. This has been left in an unrestored state, to show the method of construction used at Clandon Park.

Outside, a Maori meeting house can be seen. This was brought to Clandon by the fourth Earl of Onslow, who served as Governor of New Zealand. It is one of the oldest such buildings in existence. The Maori house is set in attractive gardens landscaped by 'Capability' Brown, which also include an Ionic temple.

In the basement of Clandon Park are a shop, a restaurant and a museum to the Queen's Royal Surrey Regiment. In the park nearby a garden centre has been established.

Claremont House, Claremont Fan Court School, Claremont Drive, Esher KT10 9LY. Telephone: 01372 467841.
Open February to November, first full weekend of month, Saturday and Sunday afternoons.

Robert Clive of India bought the old

Clandon Park is a Palladian-style house now owned by the National Trust.

Claremont House in 1768. Shortly afterwards he had it demolished, to be replaced by the present white brick building by 'Capability' Brown.

The symmetrical building is fronted by a massive portico, supported by four Corinthian columns. The entrance hall is reached by means of a flight of steps, because of the elevated basement of the house. In order not to destroy the symmetry, the kitchens were reached by a tunnel. The interior has several good pieces of work, the best being the entrance hall and the assembly hall.

The house is now a co-educational school run by Christian Scientists.

Claremont Landscape Garden, Portsmouth Road, Esher KT10 9JG. Telephone: 01372 469421. National Trust.
Open daily except Mondays, Christmas Day and New Year's Day.

Until 1975 Claremont Garden had for many years lain neglected, largely overgrown by the rhododendrons once planted as a landscape feature. The National Trust then embarked on a long programme of restoration.

Claremont is one of the earliest gardens of its kind to survive. In 1727 it was described as 'one of the noblest of any in Europe'. An amphitheatre, designed by Charles Bridgeman, covers 3 acres (1.2 hectares) and was intended to complement the pond below. It is the only surviving example of its kind in Europe. There is a grotto, a characteristic feature of eighteenth-century gardens. It was designed to appear natural and was decorated with stalactites and feldspar. On an island in the lake stands a pavilion. The oldest feature of the garden was a view of the belvedere and house (which is in separate ownership) from a bowling green. The gardens also contain a terrace, mausoleum, ninepin alley and a ha-ha – a sunken barrier which excluded animals without spoiling the view.

Claremont is not a garden of flowers but a pleasant experience in landscape design. It is

The island pavilion in the lake at Claremont Landscape Garden.

well worth a visit at any time of year. A wide selection of trees may be found throughout the grounds.

The National Trust holds special events here, with firework displays and entertainment. The public are asked to attend in costume. Details can be obtained from the Regional Office at Polesden Lacey (telephone: 01372 453401).

Croydon Old Palace, Old Palace Road, Croydon CR0 1AX. Telephone: 0181-688 2027.
Open afternoons around Easter, Spring Bank Holiday and in July. Telephone for details.

Now used as a girls' school, this palace was originally a favoured summer residence of the Archbishops of Canterbury and has considerable associations with Archbishop Laud (1573-1645). The buildings date from the late fourteenth century, with various subsequent alterations.

The fifteenth-century Great Hall, the Guardroom, Tudor chapel and Norman undercroft are among features to be seen. The

building has entertained royal guests for centuries and King James I of Scotland was held prisoner here.

Farnham Castle, Castle Hill, Farnham GU6 0AG. Telephone: 01252 721194 (castle) and 713393 (keep). Keep owned by English Heritage.
Castle open all year, Wednesday afternoons. Keep open April to September daily.

Built as a residence for the Bishops of Winchester, Farnham Castle dominates the town. Bishop Henry of Blois built the earliest structure about 1138. This consisted of a square tower on a 30 foot (10 metre) mound. Some domestic buildings were probably constructed where the present ones now stand. The whole was surrounded by an earthwork, which supports the later curtain wall. Later, in the twelfth century, the tower was dismantled and the present twenty-three sided keep built, by walling around the original motte. This and a deep well are in the care of English Heritage, which offers visitors an audio tour as part of admission.

The domestic buildings are used as a training centre by the Centre for International Briefing. The Great Hall is essentially Norman and was erected in the twelfth century. The interior has been altered during the centuries, but one of the original oak pillars can still be seen. Fine wood carving around the fireplace is probably of the Grinling Gibbons school. Beyond the hall, a spiral oak staircase leads to the upper rooms.

Upstairs, there are fine views over Farnham Park from the drawing room, which is next to the Bishop's Chapel. The library used by today's students was the study of the Bishop. A gallery runs around the top of the Great Hall linking a Tudor wing to other rooms. Through a doorway in this gallery can be seen the top of the barrel-vaulted roof of the Norman chapel below. The thickness of Norman walls is clearly visible in the downstairs kitchen. On the south side, facing the town, is the fifteenth-century asymmetrical brick tower built by Bishop Waynflete. Farnham Castle has a more domestic atmosphere than other English castles. It was occupied by the Bishops of Winchester from 1138 until 1927, when it was transferred to the new See of Guildford. It ceased to be the Bishop's residence in 1956.

Greathed Manor, Dormansland, Lingfield RH7 6PD. Telephone: 01342 832577.
Open May to September, Wednesday and Thursday afternoons.

Isolated in a parkland setting, Greathed Manor is an example of Victorian eccentricity. It was built in 1868 by Robert Kerr, author of a famous book on the English gentleman's house, for Colonel Spender Clay. The house is an odd mixture of styles. The long frontage comprises a tower in the Italian style, a Dutch gable, an English gable and a French pavilion roof.

This imposing stone house is leased by the Country Houses Association and divided into apartments for retired people used to large houses. The part open to the public comprises the entrance hall, drawing room and ballroom. The drawing room is attractively panelled, with good views over the sunken garden.

Guildford Castle, Castle Street, Guildford GU2 5BB. Telephone: 01483 444702.
Open daily, April to September.

Standing in a beautiful public garden is the impressive Norman keep of Guildford Castle. This was built about 1170 on the top of the motte, which was itself constructed soon after the Norman conquest. Together, they formed an impregnable defence.

The keep at Guildford, a royal castle, was built in the architectural style of Henry II's reign, in contrast to that at Farnham. The

Farnham Castle keep.

main entrance was at first-floor level, leaving the ground floor below as storage space. Except for a couple of Romanesque windows and a little ornamentation in the first-floor chapel, little detail remains.

Extracts from the Pipe and Liberate Rolls have been published in the Victoria County History, detailing the decoration of Guildford Castle. These included walls whitewashed outside and painted inside. Some instructions for marbling hall pillars and arches are also recorded. Today, when climbing to the top of the keep, all this is very hard to imagine.

Ham House, Ham, Richmond TW10 7RS. Telephone: 0181-940 1950. National Trust.
Open April to October, daily except Thursdays and Fridays.

One of the most outstanding examples of the Stuart period, Ham House was built in 1610 and extended in the 1670s. Much of the original furniture and decoration survives. The Dysarts and latterly the Tollemache family continued to live in the house until 1948, when ownership passed to the National Trust.

Much of the garden was restored to its seventeenth-century form in 1975. Lawns or grass paths lead to the wilderness area with its formal paths and rooms flanked by clipped hedges. The Cherry Garden has beds of lavender and santolina enclosed by low box hedging.

Hatchlands, East Clandon, Guildford GU4 7RT. Telephone: 01483 222482. National Trust.
Open April to October, daily except Mondays and Fridays.

Hatchlands was given to the National Trust in 1945, almost two hundred years after its building in the mid eighteenth century. Built for the Honourable Edward Boscawen, it contains the earliest known work of Robert Adam. Since its construction, Hatchlands has been internally altered on several occasions.

The house is entered through an Edwardian porch, on the opposite side of the building from the original entrance. In the library, which until 1889 was the drawing room, a fine Adam ceiling may be seen. The present drawing room houses a good selection of furniture and several paintings. The Boscawen Room is especially interesting, having been laid out as a small museum, charting the progress of Admiral Boscawen's career. Other rooms open to view are the morning room, garden room, music room, dining room, halls and old kitchen.

Ham House, upstream from Richmond on the river Thames.

Right: *The Norman keep of Guildford Castle stands in Castle Gardens.*

Below: *Hatchlands was the home of Admiral Boscawen.*

Loseley House, where both Elizabeth I and James I stayed.

A careful look at the outside will reveal a strange arrangement of windows at one corner. One of the three sets of windows on the south side consists of dummies, there being only two floors internally. The house is surrounded by a small attractive garden, with an interesting icehouse, perched on the edge of an old flint quarry.

Little Holland House, 40 Beeches Avenue, Carshalton SM5 3LW. Telephone: 0181-770 4781.
Open the first Sunday afternoon in each month and Bank Holiday Sunday and Monday afternoons.

Frank R. Dickinson, an admirer of the artistic and social ideals of the Pre-Raphelites such as William Morris and John Ruskin, built this house at the beginning of the twentieth century. He designed the house himself, then set about furnishing it with furniture, paintings, carvings and metalwork of his own making.

Loseley House, Loseley Park, Guildford GU3 1HS. Telephone: 01483 304440.
Open May to September, Wednesday to Saturday afternoons.

Set amid 1000 acres (400 hectares) of farmland, Loseley House, the ancestral home of the More-Molyneaux family, was built around 1562. The original accounts of the building

have been preserved, indicating the total cost to be £1640 19s 7d. The mellow stone used in the house was largely robbed from the ruins of Waverley Abbey. There was once a long wing projecting from the front of the house towards the north-west, but this was demolished around 1830.

Loseley House is still used as a family home. The Great Hall, to the right of the main entrance, contains a range of portraits and is lined with panelling said to have come from the demolished Nonsuch Palace. An inscription above the bookshelves in the library, when translated, says 'I soothe troubled minds and while away the centuries'. The family emblems of moorhens, cockatrices and mulberry trees recur throughout the house. In the drawing room, a massive carved fireplace, fashioned from a solid block of chalk, is a most amazing achievement. Another outstanding feature of the house, a selection of tapestries, is well worth seeing.

The garden may be visited, and there are tractor rides around the farm, to see one of the largest Jersey herds in Britain. Loseley Park yoghurt, cheese and ice-cream can be purchased at the Loseley shop.

Newark Priory, Pyrford. View from public footpath, road or canal towpath.

Although not directly accessible, the romantic ruins of Newark Priory are of a house of the Austin Canons, founded in the late twelfth century. A fair quantity of flint walling remains, including parts of the transept and presbytery. The ruins stand in a field beside the river.

Oakhurst Cottage, Hambledon, Godalming. Telephone: 01428 684733. National Trust.
Open end of March to end of October, Wednesday, Thursday, Saturday, Sunday and bank holiday Monday afternoons by appointment.

This very small timber-framed cottage has been restored and furnished as a cottager's dwelling, with a delightful cottage garden. Visitors are welcome, but appointments are necessary to avoid overcrowding.

Painshill Park, Portsmouth Road, Cobham KT11 1JE. Telephone: 01932 864674 or 868113.
Open early April to mid October, Sundays.

Painshill Park is an eighteenth-century landscape garden of some 158 acres (64 hectares), currently under restoration. The gardens were laid out by the Honourable Charles Hamilton between 1738 and 1773. It was well maintained by private owners until after the Second World War, when unfortunately it became neglected. A private trust was set up in 1981 to restore the garden, and now Painshill Park is returning to its former glory.

A circuit walk takes visitors through a series of emerging scenes each more surprising than the one before. The 14 acre (5.7 hectare) lake, filled by the power of a massive waterwheel, meanders through the garden, giving a perfect setting for an airy temple in Gothic style, ruined abbey,

Turkish tent, vineyard and mausoleum. The magical crystal grotto hidden away amongst the foliage on one of the islands is approached across an elegant Chinese bridge. Beyond the lake, through a picturesque valley, a castellated Gothic tower appears through the trees.

As well as a talented designer, Hamilton was a knowledgeable plantsman. While some of the most unusual trees, including the largest cedar of Lebanon in England, and shrubs he planted are still to be found in the garden, some of the shrubberies have been replanted in Hamilton's design, and give an unusual insight into eighteenth-century plantings.

The Education Trust at Painshill Park has a fully equipped education centre, with qualified teaching staff, offering a variety of services which can be tailor-made for specific school visits.

Polesden Lacey, near Dorking RH5 6BD. Telephone: 01372 458203 or 452048. National Trust.
Open early April to October, Wednesday to Sunday.

With Clandon Park and Hatchlands, Polesden Lacey is one of the three great

The Gothic temple at Painshill Park.

Polesden Lacey was built in 1824 and houses a splendid collection of fine and decorative art.

National Trust houses of Surrey. In the eight-eenth century the home of the playwright Sheridan stood on the site. This was replaced by the present building in 1824. Built for Joseph Bonsor to a design of Thomas Cubitt, it is of two storeys, surrounding an open court-yard, in a magnificent setting amid rolling woods and farmland. The interior has been totally reconstructed since it was built, but outside it retains most of its original elegance. The interior decorations and furnishings are rich and rewarding and incorporate a large collection of paintings.

The house is approached from Bookham by a long avenue and is surrounded by exten-sive gardens. These incorporate specialist gar-dens devoted to roses, irises and lavender, and theme gardens including a rock garden, sunken garden and winter garden. This last has formal hedged corridors and four iron trees, which produce crimson tassels of flowers in February.

An open-air theatre was constructed at Polesden Lacey in 1951, and plays by Shake-speare and other playwrights are performed.

Full details can be obtained from the National Trust Southern Region Office, which is based at Polesden Lacey (telephone: 01372 453401).

Royal Botanic Gardens, Kew, Richmond TW9 3AB. Telephone: 0181-940 1171.
Open daily except Christmas Day and New Year's Day.

Although Kew is the most famous garden in Britain, the primary purpose of the Royal Botanic Gardens is to act as a research institu-tion and not as a public park. Despite this, the 300 acres (120 hectares) make up one of the most pleasant open spaces in London.

There are several glasshouses around the gardens, including the famous Palm House and the Temperate House, both designed by Decimus Burton. Across the pond from the Palm House is the Princess of Wales Con-servatory. This large modern glasshouse fits unobtrusively into its surroundings and pro-vides a wide range of computer-controlled environments. These allow contrasting col-lections of plants to grow which require con-ditions ranging from those of the wet tropics

The Princess of Wales Conservatory at Kew is named after Augusta, the mother of George III.

and cloud forest to dry tropics and temperate regions.

In the south-west corner of the gardens are 47 acres (19 hectares) kept largely as natural woodland. Known as the Queen's Cottage Grounds, they were presented by Queen Victoria in 1898. Here memorable displays of snowdrops and bluebells may be seen in February and May respectively.

There are numerous buildings in Kew Gardens, apart from the Herbarium and research laboratories which are not open to the general public. Perhaps the most spectacular is the Pagoda, built in 1761 for Princess Augusta. Kew Gardens Gallery in Cambridge Cottage Garden has exhibitions of botanical illustration and interpretation of the role of Kew. A museum is housed in Kew Palace, whilst a collection of paintings occupies the Marianne North Gallery, named after their artist. There are other follies scattered across the gardens.

A large artificial lake, fed by the Thames, forms a centrepiece. Many species of waterside plants grow around the edge, with water lilies on the surface. A waterfowl collection includes black swans, Egyptian geese, shelduck and pochard.

Royal Horticultural Society's Wisley Garden, Wisley, Woking GU23 6QB. Telephone: 01483 224234.
Open Monday to Saturday. Members only on Sundays.

This garden of 240 acres (97 hectares) has been owned by the Royal Horticultural Society since 1904.

The garden has a most extensive collection of flowers, shrubs and trees. Areas of interest range from alpine glasshouse displays close by the Rock Garden, the Alpine Meadow and a series of model gardens of fruit, vegetables and herbs. There is a range of gardens created specifically with the needs of the average gardener in mind. These range from a town or suburban garden, a family garden, a scented garden for the visually impaired and a garden for the disabled to the various water features in a landscaped setting.

Facilities include a cafeteria and licensed restaurant and a picnic area near the car park, just outside the garden. There is a shop containing a most comprehensive range of books covering horticulture and botany, as well as many quality gifts. There is a well-stocked plant centre. Free wheelchairs and a route map are available.

The Savill Garden, Wick Lane, Englefield Green, Egham. Telephone: 01753 860222. *Open daily.*

This 35 acre (14 hectare) woodland garden is situated in a tranquil setting within the eastern boundary of Windsor Great Park. Spring is heralded by hosts of daffodils, masses of rhododendrons, azaleas, camellias, magnolias and much more. The hundreds of roses, herbaceous borders and countless alpines are the great feature of summer and the leaf colours and fruits of autumn rival the other seasons with a great display. Winter also has much to offer and is by no means a dull period. It is truly a garden for all seasons. An extensive new Temperate House has recently been constructed. There is a well-stocked plant centre and gift shop and self-service restaurant.

The Valley Garden, Windsor Great Park. Telephone: 01753 860222. *Open daily.*

The gardens cover some 400 acres (160 hectares) and are situated on the north bank of Virginia Water lake. Development of the area began in 1949 and it is today probably one of the finest woodland gardens in the world. It contains an unrivalled collection of rhododendrons, azaleas, camellias, magnolias and countless other spring-flowering trees and shrubs. Adjoining the woodland garden is the 10 acre (4 hectare) heather garden, which provides much colour and interest during winter and summer, the two seasons of the year when the woodland garden is less colourful.

The ruins of the monks' dorter at Waverley Abbey.

Waverley Abbey, Farnham. Telephone: 01322 863467 (Area Manager). English Heritage.
Open at all times.

Founded in 1128 by William Giffard, this first Cistercian house in Britain was colonised by monks from Aumône. Although never rich, it was one of the largest and most influential abbeys of its time. The ruins are attractively sited on the banks of the river Wey.

Westhumble Chapel, near Dorking. National Trust.
Accessible at all times.

The ruins are located opposite Chapel Farm in Westhumble Street, the lane which passes from the foot of Box Hill towards Bookham. Only parts of the east end and west wall remain. The building is thought to date from the late twelfth century and was built for those unable to cross the river to Mickleham church. A small rectangular flint building, it was given to the National Trust in 1938 by the Cubitt Estates.

Whitehall, 1 Malden Road, Cheam, Sutton SM3 8QD. Telephone: 0181-643 1236.
Open: October to March, Wednesday, Thursday and Sunday afternoons, Saturday morning and afternoon; April to September, every afternoon except Monday, plus Saturday mornings.

This white-painted weatherboarded house was built on the corner of Park Lane, around 1500, on land belonging to East Cheam Manor. Extensive alterations were made during the sixteenth century. The founder of

Whitehall is a sixteenth-century timber-framed house in Cheam.

The Cumberland Obelisk at Virginia Water.

The new Temperate House in the Savill Garden.

Phillimore Lake at Winkworth Arboretum.

Cheam School is reputed to have lived in Whitehall in the mid seventeenth century and it was the home of the Killick family for more than two hundred years. In 1978, fifteen years after being purchased by the local authority, Whitehall was opened to the public.

There is an overhanging upper floor and a two-storey Tudor porch. It is an excellent example of a vernacular timber-framed cottage, where the methods of construction can be clearly seen. The parlour hearth and nineteenth-century kitchen have been refurbished and there are displays featuring timber-framed buildings, Nonsuch Palace, Cheam pottery and Cheam School. There is a tea room and gift shop. There is a programme of changing temporary exhibitions and a variety of fairs and events throughout the year.

Winkworth Arboretum, Hascombe Road, Godalming GU8 4AD. Telephone: 01483 208477. National Trust.
Open daily.

This large wooded garden was begun by Dr Wilfred Fox in 1937. Planted over a hilly remote site near Godalming, it is particularly striking in spring, when bluebells and primroses carpet the ground, and in autumn, when the trees create a kaleidoscope of colour. In the valley are two large lakes, frequented by waterfowl. Two walks, for spring and autumn, have been laid out, from which excellent views may be had. There is a National Trust shop and tea room open in afternoons in the season, except Mondays and Fridays.

7
Museums and art galleries

Ash Vale

Royal Army Medical Corps Historical Museum, Keogh Barracks, Ash Vale, Aldershot GU12 5RQ. Telephone: 01252 340212.
Open Monday to Friday.

The museum houses more than 2500 items, giving a wide representation of the Royal Army Medical Corps, illustrating its professionalism even under the most extreme of wartime conditions.

Bagshot

Museum of the Royal Army Chaplains Department, Bagshot Park, Bagshot GU19 5PL. Telephone: 01276 412845.
Open Monday to Friday.

Housed in a Victorian building constructed in the Tudor style, this museum displays medals, uniforms, photographs, silver and church memorabilia illustrating two hundred years of work by the army chaplains. There are also diaries and items made by prisoners of war. The museum is set in 81 acres (32 hectares) of parkland.

Camberley

Regimental Museum of the Royal Logistic Corps, Princess Royal Barracks, Deepcut, Camberley GU16 6RW. Telephone: 01252 340871.
Open Monday to Saturday.

Newly designed displays mark the coming together of the Royal Corps of Transport, Royal Army Ordnance Corps, Royal Pioneer Corps and Royal Engineers Postal and Courier Service.

Staff College Museum, London Road, Camberley GU15 4NP. Telephone:01276 412650.
Open weekdays by appointment. Closed from April 1996 for two years, owing to the rebuilding of the college.

The museum provides an insight into the place where Army staff officers have been trained since 1862 and tells the history of the college and staff officers of the British Army.

Surrey Heath Museum, Surrey Heath House, Knoll Road, Camberley GU15 3HD. Telephone: 01276 686252 extension 284.
Open Tuesday to Saturday.

This small modern museum is located in the Civic Offices. It includes displays on local geology, archaeology, local building materials, place-names, highwaymen, transport, local craft industries, trade and commerce, the development of the military town, heathland ecology and the promotion of Camberley as a Victorian health resort. There is a programme of temporary exhibitions.

Carshalton

Heritage Centre, Honeywood, Honeywood Walk, Carshalton SM5 3HX. Telephone: 0181-773 4555.
Open Wednesday to Sunday and bank holiday Mondays.

The centre is devoted to the history of the London Borough of Sutton, which comprises Wallington, Carshalton, Beddington, Cheam, Sutton and Worcester Park and includes Croydon Airport. Displays include an Edwardian billiard room, a childhood room featuring Edwardian toys and games and a Tudor gallery. Exhibitions and special events are held throughout the year. There is an art gallery, tea room and gift shop.

Caterham

East Surrey Museum, 1 Stafford Road, Caterham CR3 6JG. Telephone: 01883 340275.
Open Sunday afternoons, Wednesdays and Saturdays.

This museum is run by a group of volunteers and was first opened in 1980. The displays cover the local history, archaeology,

*Chatley Heath
Semaphore
Tower was used
to send
messages
between
Portsmouth and
the Admiralty
in London.*

crafts and natural history of east Surrey. A large relief map on the wall charts the distribution of archaeological sites by the use of coloured lights.

Displays are changed about every three months, but the museum's store of geological specimens, fossils and all archaeological finds relating to the area are available for study purposes when not on show.

Chertsey

Chertsey Museum, The Cedars, 33 Windsor Street, Chertsey KT16 8AT. Telephone: 01932 565764.
Open Saturdays and afternoons from Tuesday to Friday.

Situated in an attractive Regency town house, Chertsey Museum offers a stimulating variety of displays, including the local history and archaeology of the Borough of Runnymede, the Matthews Collection of eighteenth- and nineteenth-century costume, clocks, ceramics and glass. It also has a lively and varied temporary exhibition and events programme.

Cobham

Chatley Heath Semaphore Tower, Pointers Road, Cobham KT11 1PQ. Telephone: 01932 862762. Access from Old Lane, Wisley, off southbound A3.
Open late March to early October, Saturday, Sunday and bank holiday afternoons; also Wednesday afternoons during Surrey school holidays.

A twenty-minute walk through heath and woodland brings the visitor to this ex-Admiralty naval semaphore station. The tower was built in 1822 as one of fourteen semaphore stations between Portsmouth and the Admiralty in London. Each station, visible from the next, was surmounted by a semaphore signalling mast and was used to send messages visually, before the days of electronic telegraph. The towers were usually staffed by elderly naval personnel, nearing retirement. When in operation, it was possible for a message to be transmitted along the entire line in fifteen minutes.

It ceased to serve its original function in

The Mortuary Chapel of G. F. Watts at Compton was designed by his wife and has a remarkable Art Nouveau interior.

1848 and proved difficult to adapt for other purposes owing to its isolated location and lack of amenities. It was tenanted until 1963 but for many years the tower remained empty and was reduced to a burnt-out shell by vandals in 1984. To celebrate their centenary, Surrey County Council restored the tower in 1989 and opened it to the public. There are exhibitions about the tower and signalling, working models, a shop and a room giving information about walking the Surrey countryside. There are stunning views across London and the south-east, for those climbing to the rooftop, which has telescopes.

Cobham Bus Museum, Redhill Road, Cobham KT11 1EF. Telephone: 01932 864078.
Open last Sunday in each month.

Cobham Bus Museum is housed in a huge garage on the south side of the A245 between Cobham and Byfleet. Outside the museum are many old road signs, bus stops and street furniture, including old AA call boxes. More road signs as well as bus tickets, timetables, posters and other transport memorabilia are housed inside.

The main feature of the museum is the large collection of London buses dating back over many decades and displayed in a working garage atmosphere. This is a museum for the enthusiast, where members of the London Bus Preservation Group work to restore the old vehicles. Many of the buses are in excellent condition and full working order.

Compton

Watts Gallery, Down Lane, Compton, Guildford GU3 1DQ. Telephone: 01483 810235.
Open afternoons except Thursdays, plus Wednesday and Saturday mornings.

George Frederic Watts (1817-1904) was a popular Victorian artist – a painter of portraits and allegories and a sculptor. The gallery was purpose-built in 1903 and houses a comprehensive collection of his work. Nearby is the remarkable Mortuary Chapel, designed by his wife Mary, also an artist. It is a circular building dating from 1896-8 and covered in Celtic and Art Nouveau decoration.

Egham Museum is in the Literary Institute of the town.

Croydon

Croydon Clocktower, Katharine Street, Croydon CR9 1ET. Telephone: 0181-760 5400.

Open every afternoon.

Croydon Clocktower is a new cultural centre which has been developed in Croydon's old Victorian town hall. The building has been completely refurbished and includes a central library, exhibition gallery, living history museum, collection of Chinese pottery, cinema, function hall, arts workshops, cafe and shop.

The exhibition gallery is used for a varied programme of touring exhibitions ranging from art to science fiction, literature and virtual reality.

Lifetimes, the living history museum, is based on the lives of local people and is a visually exciting display of real objects and local memories, enhanced by the use of interactive technology. It reflects the development of the community and its cultural diversity.

Dorking

Dorking and District Museum, The Old Foundry, 62a West Street, Dorking RH4 1BS. Telephone: 01306 743821.

Open Wednesday and Thursday afternoons; Saturday mornings and afternoons.

This small museum displays many items of local interest, such as agricultural and domestic bygones, the Lord Ashcombe's collection of minerals and chalk fossils, cased birds, and oil and watercolour paintings by local artists.

The library contains an extensive collection of photographs, prints, books, press cuttings, ratebooks, sales particulars and maps of the area, of considerable benefit to researchers of local history and to family historians.

Egham

Egham Museum, Literary Institute, High Street, Egham TW20 9EW. Telephone: 01344 843047.

Open Thursdays and Saturdays.

This small museum houses collections relating to the local history, archaeology and art of the Egham area. Souvenir china and clockmaking are among the more unusual topics covered.

The Picture Gallery, Royal Holloway and Bedford New College, Egham Hill, Egham TW20 0EX. Telephone: 01784 443045 or 443046.

Open by arrangement.

The gallery displays Victorian art, and its contents are detailed in an illustrated catalogue, *Victorian Taste*.

Ewell

Bourne Hall Museum, Spring Street, Ewell KT17 1UF. Telephone: 0181-394 1734.

Open Monday to Saturday.

This small museum relating to the Epsom and Ewell area is housed in the dome of a modern cultural complex. Exhibits include Victorian machinery and an early fire-engine. There are archaeological displays covering Roman Ewell and the lost palace of Nonsuch. Several cases illustrate local life over the last hundred years. National personalities are commemorated, such as the late nineteenth-century Prime Minister Lord Rosebery and Chuter Ede, the Labour education minister. Exhibitions, changing every four months, explore local history themes in a lively way.

Bourne Hall also contains an art gallery in the foyer, with changing exhibitions and a collectors' library.

Farnham

Museum of Farnham, Willmer House, 38 West Street, Farnham GU9 7DX. Telephone: 01252 715094.

Open Tuesday to Saturday.

The Museum of Farnham is housed in an elegant Georgian town house with innovative displays which allow the visitor to 'meet the past face to face'. All aspects of local history are well represented in this award-winning museum, including memorabilia of local personalities such as William Cobbett, the radical politician, the inventor J. H. Knight and Baden-Powell, founder of the Scouting movement. In addition to the main displays, topical temporary exhibitions are also staged. At the rear are a delightful walled garden and additional gallery.

Godalming

Godalming Museum, 109a High Street, Godalming GU7 1AQ. Telephone: 01483 426510.

Open Tuesday to Saturday.

Situated opposite the town's 1814 town hall, known as 'The Pepperpot', this museum is housed in a fifteenth-century town house.

Displays relate to the local history of Godalming, the first town in Britain to be lit by electric street lights. There is a room dedicated to the architect and gardener team Edwin Lutyens and Gertrude Jekyll, and outside is a restored garden in Miss Jekyll's style. A display tells the life story of George Phillips, a local man who was wireless operator on the *Titanic*. Another expands on the life of General Sir James Oglethorpe, founder of the colony of Georgia in America. There are also displays of local geology, archaeology and old businesses of the area.

Guildford

The Brooking Architectural Museum Trust, Woodhay, White Lane, Guildford GU4 8PU. Telephone: 01483 504555.

Open by appointment.

Part of a remarkable collection of architectural features assembled by Charles Brooking, the museum includes such objects as window frames, door and window ironmongery, staircases and fireplaces, some drawn from the grandest of private homes, some from the often neglected commercial sector and featuring much from the humble urban terrace or rural cottage of south-east England. Attempts are being made to establish a permanent collection in central Guildford.

Left: *Lowfield Heath Windmill at Charlwood is being restored to working order.*

Below: *The Magna Carta Memorial at Runnymede.*

Guildford House Gallery, 155 High Street, Guildford GU1 3AJ. Telephone: 01483 444740.
Open Tuesday to Saturday.

Built in 1660, Guildford House is now an important art gallery. The building has a fine carved wooden staircase, panelling and plaster ceilings. A temporary exhibition programme ranges from children's art to fine historical and contemporary paintings and craftwork. Also on display is a selection from the borough's art collection including pastel portraits by Guildford-born artist John Russell RA (1745-1806). There is a tea room and shop.

Guildford Museum, Castle Arch, Guildford GU1 3SX. Telephone: 01483 444750.
Open Monday to Saturday.

The Surrey Archaeological Society first established a museum at Castle Arch in 1898. Since 1933 it has been the sole responsibility of the local authority. The most interesting internal feature of this attractive building is a large chalk fireplace of 1630. The collections largely comprise items illustrating the local history and archaeology of Surrey. Finds included in the collection range from palaeolithic hand axes, through Roman remains, to objects from the Saxon cemetery at Guildown. An important display of monastic finds can be seen, including those from the Dominican friary at Guildford and from Chertsey Abbey. Evidence of the glassmaking and ironworking industries can be viewed. Cast and wrought ironwork fills one room, much of it being of a domestic nature. Rural crafts are displayed in another room. An important part of the collections relates to needlework and embroidery. A larger exhibit is the old town fire-engine of 1863. The life and work of Lewis Carroll, who died a short distance from the museum, are also covered.

Guildhall, High Street, Guildford. Telephone: 01483 444035.
Open Tuesday and Thursday afternoons for guided tours.

One of Guildford's most famous landmarks, with a magnificent clock overhang-ing the street, this Tudor building with a seventeenth-century frontage contains borough treasures and civic insignia.

University of Surrey Library Gallery, Stag Hill, Guildford. Telephone: 01483 300800.
Open Monday to Friday; also Saturday and Sunday afternoons in term time.

This art gallery with regularly changing exhibitions specialises in work by contemporary artists.

Haslemere

The Educational Museum, 78 High Street, Haslemere GU27 2LA. Telephone: 01428 642112.
Open Tuesday to Saturday.

This museum was founded in 1888, when Sir Jonathan Hutchinson, an eminent surgeon, set up a small private museum in an outbuilding at his house. The museum moved to Museum Hill in the town in 1895, but the building has since been demolished. The collection was moved to the present building in 1926. Even as early as 1897 a curator was employed to care for the collections.

The galleries are approached through an entrance hall, where displays of local natural history are changed seasonally. Of the main galleries, the first deals with geology, particularly its relationship to the Wealden landscape. The zoology gallery emphasises the classification of vertebrates, using a host of examples, and there is a display looking at the classification of plants. A specially built room houses a fine collection of British birds.

In the archaeology and history collections a time chart around the walls places special emphasis on the length of each archaeological period. Temporary exhibitions are held in the Haslemere Room, Lecture Hall or new Waverley Room, whilst a glass-fronted hive in the wall allows a close view of working bees. A programme of changing exhibitions is held and there is a joint Haslemere Museum and National Trust shop. There are extensive grounds open during the summer months, around which a nature trail is planned.

Haxted Mill is on the river Eden.

Haxted

Haxted Mill, Haxted Road, Edenbridge, Kent TN8 6PU. Telephone: 01732 862914.
Open Easter to end of September, daily except Mondays, but open bank holiday Mondays.

Haxted Mill is a unique combination of a working watermill and a museum of functional mill machinery with the emphasis on the history, development and multiple uses of water power. The double-fronted mill was built in two halves, the first around 1580 and the second in 1794. It has been fully restored and includes a picture gallery and three floors of exhibits and artefacts. There are walks along the River Eden and a brasserie overlooking the river.

Kingston upon Thames

Kingston Museum, Wheatfield Way, Kingston upon Thames KT1 2PS. Telephone: 0181-546 5386.
Open daily except Wednesdays and Sundays.

This well-presented museum has collections relating to the local history of the area,

its archaeology and folk life. It also has displays of Martinware art pottery and a collection of the work of Eadweard Muybridge (1830-1904), a photographer important for his pioneering work in photographic studies of motion and in motion-picture projection. There is a regular programme of temporary exhibitions in the first-floor art gallery, which is fully accessible by lift.

The archives and local history resource collection of books, pamphlets, maps and illustrations may be consulted at the North Kingston Centre, Richmond Road, Kingston upon Thames KT2 5PE (closed Saturdays and Sundays).

Leatherhead

Leatherhead Museum of Local History, Hampton Cottage, 64 Church Street, Leatherhead KT22 8DP. Telephone: 01372 277611.
Open April to December, Thursday afternoons, Friday morning and Saturdays.

Hampton Cottage is a seventeenth-century timber-framed cottage set in a conservation area and was opened as a museum in 1980 by the Leatherhead and District Local History Society. Displays cover the local history of Ashtead, Bookham, Fetcham and Leatherhead and include a collection of Ashtead pottery. Temporary exhibitions are mounted periodically.

Mitcham

Wandle Industrial Museum, Ravensbury Hill, Morden Road, Mitcham. Telephone: 0181-648 0127.
Open Wednesday afternoons, also the afternoon of the first Sunday in each month.

Established in 1983, the museum reflects the heritage of the river Wandle. The display concentrates on the snuff, tobacco and textile industries. Particular homage is paid to William Morris and Arthur Liberty.

Redhill

Royal Earlswood Hospital Museum, Brighton Road, Redhill RH1 6JL. Telephone: 01737 763591.
Open at any reasonable time by appointment.

This museum deals with all aspects of the hospital's history. It is divided into eight sections dealing with the development and early his-

tory, building, engineering and farming, entertainment, education, training, nursing and medical matters and finance. Items from Netherne Hospital, a large psychiatric institution at Coulsdon, which closed in 1994 after eighty-six years, have been incorporated into the collection.

Reigate

Fire Brigades of Surrey Preservation Trust, Surrey Fire and Rescue Service, St Davids, Wray Park Road, Reigate RH2 0EJ. Telephone: 01737 242444.
Open by appointment on weekdays and mornings at weekends.

The collection covers the history of firefighting in the old county of Surrey from local brigades up to modern times.

Reigate Priory Museum, Reigate Priory Middle School, Bell Street, Reigate RH2 7RL. Telephone: 01737 245065.
Open every Saturday afternoon; Wednesday afternoons in term time.

The museum's collection includes domestic and local history items and costumes. Changing exhibitions cover a wide range of subjects and feature loaned material.

Leatherhead Museum of Local History is in Church Street.

Richmond-upon-Thames

Museum of Richmond, Old Town Hall, Whittaker Avenue, Richmond TW9 1TP. Telephone: 0181-332 1141.

Open all year, Tuesday to Saturday; also Sunday afternoons from May to October.

This exciting museum tells the story of Richmond, Ham, Petersham and Kew from prehistoric times to the present day. Displays range from stone age arrowheads to a life-size model of Queen Elizabeth I made by local schoolchildren. The displays are complemented by explanatory text, maps, models and audio-visual displays. There are detailed models of two buildings of medieval Richmond, Shene Charterhouse and Richmond Palace. The displays look at the river, royal parks, theatres and the many residents who have shaped this Thames-side town. Special temporary exhibitions are staged and there is a museum shop and a coffee shop.

Ripley

Ripley Local History Museum, High Street, Ripley. Telephone enquiries: 01483 222107 or 222233.

Open Saturday mornings and some Sunday mornings; also Saturday afternoons in summer.

This small museum was opened in 1993 by the Send and Ripley History Society in the Tudor-style National Westminster Bank building of 1930, which was moved in its entirety 600 yards (550 metres) to the present site near the village hall. The exhibits concentrate on local features and artefacts and include a display of clay-pipe bowls.

Shere

Shere Museum, The Malt House, Shere GU5 9HS. Telephone: 01483 203245.

Open Easter to end of September, daily except Wednesdays and Saturdays.

This wide-ranging museum of mainly Victorian and later bygones and local history also stages temporary exhibitions.

Staines

Spelthorne Museum, Market Square, Staines TW18 4RH. Telephone: 01784 461804.

Open Wednesday, Friday and Saturday afternoons.

Run by volunteers, Spelthorne Museum houses an interesting range of objects connected with archaeology and local history. In addition to Roman remains discovered in the area, there are displays on local industries and the fire service, including a 1738 fire-engine.

Tilford

Rural Life Centre, Old Kiln Museum, Reeds Road, Tilford, Farnham, GU10 2DL. Telephone: 01272 792300 or 795571.

Open April to September, Wednesday to Sunday and bank holiday Mondays.

The Rural Life Centre is an extensive collection of items related to rural life, assembled by Madge and Henry Jackson and set in 10 acres (4 hectares) of fields, woodland and barns. It comprises a large selection of implements and devices marking over one hundred years of farming. Displays include farming through the seasons, local hop growing, tools, crafts and rural industries, the social history of village life and rural life during the 1930s and Second World War. There is an arboretum, narrow-gauge railway and the story of J. Gibbs Ltd, a company which evolved from builders of horse-drawn vehicles to motor distributors. The last Sunday in July is Rustic Sunday when over twenty different crafts people demonstrate their skills. They are accompanied by traditional children's entertainment, side shows, an accordion band and Morris dancers. There are picnic areas and a café, and facilities for the disabled, with easy access. Schools, youth groups and adult groups (pre-booked) are welcome.

Weybridge

Brooklands Museum, Brooklands Road, Weybridge KT13 0QN. Telephone: 01932 857381.

Open Tuesday to Sunday.

Original Brooklands racing cars, motorcycles and bicycles are on display and, as well as many of the old buildings, the steepest section of the old banked track is preserved. The museum also tells the story of eighty-six years of aircraft production and includes a Wellington bomber rescued from Loch Ness. The new 'Fastest on Earth' exhi-

The petrol pagoda at Brooklands Museum.

bition tells the story of record breaking at Brooklands.

Elmbridge Museum, Church Street, Weybridge KT13 8DE. Telephone: 01932 843573.
Open Saturdays, and weekday afternoons, except Wednesdays.
This is a modern museum, reopened after refurbishment in early 1996, illustrating the history, costume, archaeology and natural history of the Elmbridge district. The displays and exhibitions range from mammoths' teeth to televisions, and from handcarts to 'hot pants'. Finds from the demolished Oatlands Palace are included in the collections. There is a museum shop.

Wimbledon
Wimbledon Lawn Tennis Museum, All England Club, Church Road, Wimbledon SW19 5AE. Telephone: 0181-946 6131.
Open Tuesday to Saturday and Sunday afternoons.

The museum displays fashion, trophies, memorabilia and mementoes which illustrate the history of lawn tennis. There is also a racket maker's workshop.

Wonersh
British Red Cross Museum and Archives, Barnett Hill, Wonersh, Guildford GU5 0RF. Telephone: 01483 898595.
Open weekdays by appointment.
The museum is devoted to the history of the British Red Cross Society from its foundation, including medical and nursing equipment, medals, badges, uniforms and photographs.

8
Industrial archaeology

Today Surrey has very little heavy industry, but this was not always so. Ironmaking, glassmaking, limeburning, brickmaking and gunpowder manufacture are a few of the activities once practised in this small county.

Before the industrial revolution industry was on a much smaller scale than in modern times. It was more practical for processes such as ironmaking to take place in areas with the most raw materials to hand. Ironstone, from which ore is extracted, occurs widely in the Weald. There was plenty of timber for the furnaces and water power to work the hammers which beat the wrought iron, and so this was the ideal location. Hammer ponds, such as those at Abinger, provided the necessary power and are the most conspicuous feature of the iron industry remaining today.

Far fewer remains of glassmaking are to be found. This was concentrated in the south-west of the county, especially around Chiddingfold, where production continued until the end of the sixteenth century. Archaeological investigation has revealed much information about these sites.

The extractive industries have left a more obvious mark on Surrey. The scars of the old chalk quarries are now a notable landmark. Chalk is still quarried at Oxted, as are sand between Dorking and Godstone, and fuller's earth around Redhill. Gravel extraction is a major industry in northern Surrey.

Most of the Surrey brickworks are situated on the Weald Clay. Some are now disused, such as that at Newdigate, where the site is crossed by a public footpath and retains some of the buildings associated with brick production. Here the clay pits form two lakes. Near Cranleigh a tile works still operates, manufacturing hand-made tiles, many of which decorate the exterior walls of Surrey cottages.

Watermills were used for a variety of purposes; grinding corn, making wire, gunpowder making, fulling and other processes of the woollen industry, and leather manufacture. Few survive intact today, many having been converted to houses. Those that do include Haxted and Shalford. The Tillingbourne, a small river flowing from Leith Hill to Shalford, and the Wandle, another short river from Carshalton to the Thames, were lined with mills in their heyday.

Communications have played an important part in the development of the county. Until the nineteenth century Surrey was relatively remote, communication being hampered by appalling roads. Since that time a dense network of roads and railways has developed, largely radiating from London, and bringing about the suburbanisation of large tracts of northern Surrey. Many old signs, milestones and bridges now add to the industrial archaeology of the county.

Betchworth Chalk Quarries, Betchworth.
These extensive old quarries, together with the neighbouring Brockham Quarry, are a major landmark on the North Downs, seen when approaching from the south. They can be reached either from the B2032 at Betchworth station or via the North Downs Way, which passes through the complex. Quarries are dangerous places even when disused. Visitors should not climb any of the surviving structures and should keep away from the cliff faces.

Frimley Aqueduct carries the Basingstoke Canal across the London to Southampton railway.

Near the station are the remains of several quarry buildings and two groups of kilns. One group is surmounted by four circular charging towers, the other by two brick flues. A rare, separate, very tall brick kiln can be seen from some distance. Also visible are remains of quarry railway tracks and viaducts.

At the nearby Brockham Quarries, accessible by footpath through a farm from the A25 at TQ 196505, are the remains of a different series of kilns, built to a design patented by Alfred Bishop in the late nineteenth century. They were used until the 1930s. Hearthstone was also mined here, and bricks were produced early in the twentieth century. Between the quarry and the road is an isolated group of old quarrymen's cottages.

Chilworth Gunpowder Mills, Chilworth, Guildford (OS 186: TQ 039480, TQ 025475, TQ 028475).

A quiet country footpath leads eastwards from Blacksmith Lane, Chilworth, through woodland alongside the river Tillingbourne, to the site of a series of old gunpowder mills. The industry survived here from the seventeenth century until 1920, despite some serious explosions, which killed several people.

The channels through which water was directed to power the mills can still be seen, as can several millstones and the thick concrete walls of the buildings. The reason for the absence of a front wall and roof is that these

were of flimsy construction so that the force of any explosion would be dissipated and the mill would better withstand the blast. Across the fields, beyond the woods, can be seen a very odd-looking group of cottages. They have thick concrete walls projecting from the front of the terrace, indicating that they have been converted from old gunpowder mills.

Cobham Mill, Mill Road, Cobham KT11 3AI. Telephone: 01932 864393.
Open April to October on the second Sunday afternoon of each month, and for private parties throughout the year.

The present watermill on the river Mole was rebuilt in 1822 and has been fully restored. Visitors can see demonstrations of grinding. The low-breast waterwheel drives a pair of stones and a sack hoist.

Ewhurst Windmill, Ewhurst, Cranleigh (OS 187: TQ 077427).

800 feet (244 metres) above sea level, overlooking the Weald from Hurtwood, stands a four-storey brick tower mill. Now converted into a house and well hidden by trees, this mill was built around 1840 and ceased working in 1885.

Frimley Aqueduct, Frimley, Camberley (OS 186: SU 893564).

Off the B3012, near the railway bridge at Frimley Green, stands this impressive four-

Gomshall Mill, near Guildford, houses recently restored machinery, a craft gallery and a tea shop.

arch aqueduct, carrying the Basingstoke Canal over the London to Southampton railway. Built of blue engineering brick in 1900, it had a stop lock built at each end in 1940, in case it was bombed.

Gomshall Mill, Gomshall, Guildford GU5 9LB. Telephone: 01486 412433.
Open daily.

There has been a watermill on this site on the river Tillingbourne since at least 1086, when it was recorded in Domesday Book. In the eighteenth and nineteenth centuries it was one of the most important corn mills in the area. It ceased commercial operation in 1952 and the buildings fell into disuse. Restoration commenced in 1964 and now the beautifully restored mill houses quaint and unusual gift shops and a restaurant famous for its watercress soup, trout and cream teas. Trout swim in the river, which still flows below the mill building, although the millpond has become a garden. There are two waterwheels: the larger, partially restored, is 18 feet (5.5 metres) in

diameter and 6 feet (1.8 metres) wide; the smaller, made of oak, is a replica of an eleventh-century design and is used to generate electricity.

Guildford Crane and Treadmill, Guildford (OS 186: SU 994494).

On the waterside near Guildford Town Bridge, housed in a tiled and weatherboarded shed, are a crane and treadmill of the seventeenth or eighteenth century. The crane was used to unload barges on the quayside at Guildford until 1908. Fitted with a chain and hook, it was powered by the 18 foot (5.5 metres) wheel. The whole installation is in excellent condition.

Lowfield Heath Windmill, Russ Hill, Charlwood. Telephone: 01293 862646.
The exterior may be viewed at any time; the upper floors are open on summer Sunday afternoons. Special visits by arrangement.

This post mill originally stood near Gatwick Airport but has been moved and re-erected at a site near to Gatwick Zoo and is being restored to full working order.

Outwood Common Windmill, Outwood Common, near Redhill RH1 5PW. Telephone: 01342 843458.

Open Easter to end of October, Sunday and bank holiday Monday afternoons.

Outwood Mill is the oldest working windmill in England. It is a post mill with a brick roundhouse, weatherboarded top and full complement of sails. It was built in 1665 by Thomas Budgen, a miller in the nearby village of Nutfield. The king post on which the mill is balanced is made of oak. The mill is 39 feet (12 metres) tall, with each pair of sails measuring 59 feet (18 metres). The whole mill can be turned to face the wind using the tailpole, which projects through the steps. When in the required position, the steps can be lowered to act as an anchor.

From 1790 until 1960 another windmill stood next to Outwood Mill. It was built following an argument between two brothers to 'take the wind out of the other's sails'. Ironically, it was blown down during a storm.

Reigate Heath Windmill, Reigate.

One of three windmills in the Reigate area, this mill, in Flanchford Road, was built in 1765. Like Outwood, a few miles away, it is a post mill in excellent condition. The mill stopped working around 1870. About ten years later the roundhouse was converted into a chapel, a function it still serves today. The tailpole, by which the mill was turned into the wind, is still in position. There is a fine set of sails although these have been fixed. It is a Grade Two listed building.

Shalford Mill, Shalford, Guildford. National Trust.

Open daily.

This attractive eighteenth-century watermill on the tiny river Tillingbourne is usually open to the public. It is a timber-framed building, with lower walls of brick. The side walls are tile-hung. The mill was originally owned by the Godwin-Austin family and used for grinding corn until 1914, when it fell into disuse. By 1932 it had become very dilapidated but an anonymous group of preservationists, known as Ferguson's Gang, raised money to restore it, after having been given the property by the owner. Later it was presented to the National Trust. Much of the mill machinery remains intact and may be viewed in one part of the building. The rest of Shalford Mill has been converted into a house. The mill is four storeys high, and one of about thirty mills that once lined the banks of the Tillingbourne.

Surrey Iron Railway, Merstham (OS 187: TQ 290534).

Opened in 1803 between Wandsworth and Croydon, the Surrey Iron Railway was the first public railway in the world. The wagons

Outwood Common Windmill is the oldest working one in England.

The short rails from the first public railway in the world are displayed at Merstham.

were drawn by horses. In 1805 it was extended south to Merstham, near Redhill, mainly to carry stone from the important mines in the area. The railway was closed in 1838.

There are several remains of this railway around Merstham. A short length of track is displayed in a small public garden in the centre of the village. Two brick bridges are preserved further north, near Hooley, and several sections of embankment and cutting remain.

Town Mill, Millmead, Guildford.

This three-storey red-brick mill was built in 1766. It was adapted to house a waterworks in 1901 and has now been converted into a studio theatre by the neighbouring Yvonne Arnaud Theatre.

Wey Valley bridges

There is an attractive series of medieval bridges spanning the river Wey, south of Guildford. They are believed to have origins in the thirteenth century. At Eashing (SU 946438) is a double medieval bridge, joined into one by a stone causeway. The other bridges are at Elstead (SU 905438), Unstead (SU 993454) and two at Tilford (SU 872435 and 874434).

Wray Common Windmill, Reigate.

This mill lies on the east side of Wray Common, a large open space between Reigate and Merstham, on the Croydon Road. It is a brick tower mill, painted black, with a white top. The building has pointed windows and a Palladian doorcase. Today, the mill is a private house and the sails are missing. It was built in 1824.

The gardens at Busbridge Lakes.

9
Other places to visit

Beaver Waterworld and Reptile Zoo, Waylands Farm, Approach Road, Tatsfield TN16 2JT. Telephone: 01959 577707.
Open daily.
This small collection includes alligators, giant pythons, fish, birds, pets and much more.

Birdworld, Holt Pound, Farnham GU10 4LD. Telephone: 01420 22992.
Open daily.
Just across the border in Hampshire, near Farnham, the bird park comprises gardens, woodland and parks containing birds of many kinds, including flamingos, parrots, pelicans, penguins and vultures.

Blackwater Valley Visitor Centre, Frimley Business Park, Frimley, Camberley GU16 5SG. Telephone: 01276 686615.
Open Monday to Friday mornings; also Sunday afternoons from June to September.
Information on activities and places to visit in the Blackwater Valley is provided by this environmental resource centre.

Bocketts Farm Park, Young Street, Fetcham, Leatherhead KT22 9BS. Telephone: 01372 363764.
Open daily.
This is a working family farm in a picturesque historic setting on the slopes of the North Downs. There are plenty of animals to be seen, including young ones in a large covered area. The farm grows many crops and the farming year is punctuated by lambing, shearing, haymaking and harvesting. There are children's play areas and refreshment facilities. Home-made food is served in an eighteenth-century barn.

Burpham Court Farm Park, Clay Lane, Jacobs Well, Guildford GU4 7NA. Telephone: 01483 576089.
Open daily.
This is a conservation centre for endangered breeds of farm livestock, set in 76 acres (30 hectares), with wildlife habitats, farm and riverside walks, picnic and play area and a pets' corner. Lambing can be watched in spring. There are angling facilities, a tea room and gift shop.

Busbridge Lakes Waterfowl and Gardens, Hambledon Road, Godalming GU8 4AY. Telephone: 01483 421955.
Open at bank holiday periods; telephone for details.
40 acres (16 hectares) of parkland and three lakes provide a sanctuary for hundreds of rare waterfowl, pheasants and peafowl of a hundred different species. This private collection has been assembled to provide a breeding place for the birds and includes a heritage garden. The present house was originally the stables of Busbridge Hall, which was demolished in 1906. The grounds have an interesting group of follies and caves and are landscaped with many trees and bridges.

Chapel Farm and Animal Trail, Westhumble, Dorking RH5 6AY. Telephone: 01306 882865.
Open mid February to November.
This is a 200 acre (80 hectare) farm with a numbered farm trail, animals and an interesting range of farm buildings. There are trailer rides, woodland and field walks, picnic sites and covered areas.

Chessington World of Adventures, Chessington KT9 2NE. Telephone: 01372 727227.
Open pre-Easter to late October; telephone for times and further information.
Chessington World of Adventures is the most visited theme park in southern England. Its thrilling rides include Rameses Revenge, Dragon River and the Vampire, and there is a

special attraction just for children – Toytown. In addition there are crazy entertainers, rare animals and a Big Top spectacular show, all set in magnificently themed lands.

Countryways Experience, Springbok Estate, Alfold, Cranleigh GU6 8EX. Telephone 01403 752270. Off A281 south of Guildford. *Open daily.*

The attractions here include a wide range of farm animals, a large ornamental water garden and an expanse of ancient woodland.

Deen City Farm, 1 Batsworth Road, off Church Road, Mitcham. Telephone: 0181-648 1461. *Open daily.*

This city farm features a variety of livestock, a riding school and organic horticulture. Refreshments and farm produce are available.

Denbies Wine Estate, London Road, Dorking RH5 6AA. Telephone: 01306 876616. *Open daily.*

England's largest wine estate, set in 250 acres (100 hectares) of countryside, Denbies has 300,000 vines, capable of producing more than one million bottles of wine. The courtyard-style, flint-clad château buildings house two state-of-the-art educational theatres explaining the art of winemaking. One audio-visual display follows every aspect of wine production through the seasons, while another has the world's first three-dimensional time-lapse film, showing the growth of the vine from bud burst to picking. Moving carriages transport visitors through the working winery and there is the opportunity to taste the produce. 7 miles (11 km) of footpaths provide ample walking through the estate and there are refreshment facilities and a shop.

Gatwick Zoo, Russ Hill, Charlwood RH6 0EG. Telephone: 01293 862312. *Open daily.*

The zoo is set on the Surrey/Sussex border, 4 miles (6 km) from Gatwick Airport. It mainly comprises a large collection of birds, ranging from storks, flamingos, penguins and parrots to finches. Among the mammals wallabies, mara, monkeys and lemurs are to be found. All are housed in large, planted enclosures. The zoo claims to have one of the best monkey islands in Britain, with its own monkey house, waterfall and oak tree. There is also a large tropical garden. A café, gift shop and picnic area make for a comfortable visit. For children who tire of the animals, an adventure playground has been established.

Godstone Farm, Tilburstow Hill Road, Godstone RH9 8LX. Telephone: 01883 742546. *Open March to October, daily.*

At Godstone Farm, set in 40 acres (16 hectares) of beautiful countryside, children can meet a variety of animals and enjoy learning a lot about them. Displays include a dairy, beekeeping and spinning. There are adventure play areas, sandpits, a gift shop and tea room.

Great Cockrow Railway, Hardwick Lane, Lyne, Chertsey. Telephone: 01932 228950 or 565474. *Open May to October, Sunday afternoons.*

This 7¼ inch (184 mm) gauge passenger-carrying miniature railway first opened to the public in 1964. The constantly growing network of tracks offers a choice of two regular routes, which are controlled by a comprehensive signalling system. With six stations, a tunnel and a viaduct, this is just like a full-scale railway, only smaller.

Hogs Back Brewery, Manor Farm, The Street, Tongham GU10 1DE. Telephone: 01252 783000. *Open daily.*

This working independent brewery in a building of 1768 provides brewery tours, a retail shop and off-licence and traditional fare.

Horton Park Children's Farm, Horton Lane, Epsom KT19 8PT. Telephone: 01372 743984. *Open daily.*

Here there are plenty of friendly animals, indoor and outdoor play areas, a sandpit, a straw pit, ride-on toys and a mini-maze.

The Old Farm at Shere, Durfold House, Shere, Guildford GU5 9HF. Telephone: 01483 202976.

Open every weekday throughout the year, and weekends from May to August.

This complete farm experience ranges from lambs to demonstrations of shearing, spinning, weaving, ropemaking, sowing corn and milling flour. Guided tours and demonstrations are given.

Runnymede, Egham.

Open at all times.

By the Thames near Egham lies a large grassy expanse which gained a place in history on 15th June 1215. For it was here, at Runnymede, that King John signed Magna Carta, recognising the rights and privileges of the barons, church and freemen. This lifted the threat of civil war and is commemorated by a memorial erected by the American Bar Association. Nearby, and beyond a belt of trees, is a simple white memorial stone, 10 feet (3 metres) by 5 feet (1.5 metres), dedicated to President John F. Kennedy. It is approached over stone setts through woodland. On Coopers Hill, above the meadows, stands another memorial flanked by trees. Designed by Sir Edward Maufe, architect of Guildford Cathedral, it records the names of twenty thousand aircrew killed between 1939 and 1945.

At the west end of Runnymede, which is in the care of the National Trust, are two lodges by Lutyens. One of these is used as a tearoom and houses some small exhibits relating to the area. Here one can view a plan of Egham Racecourse, which occupied these meadows in 1828. Nearby, river cruises are available, taking more than half an hour to pass through the area. The Thames Path follows the river here and Langham Ponds Site of Special Scientific Interest preserves one of the best sites for wetland plants in Surrey.

Thorpe Park, Staines Road, Chertsey KT16 8PN. Telephone: 01932 569393. Near junctions 11 and 13 on the M25.

Open Easter to late October, daily.

Thorpe Park was Britain's first theme park, opened in 1979. Popular attractions include Loggers Leap, the highest log flume in the United Kingdom, Depth Charge, Thunder River and the Flying Fish family coaster. Visitors can head for new adventures in Ranger County, explore the legend of the Rangers on Mr Rabbit's Tropical Travels, take to the jungle on Miss Hippo's Fungle Safari or reach for the sky on Mr Monkey's Swinging Banana Ride. Splashtacular, Britain's first stunt spectacular, provides thirty minutes of thrills, including an 85 foot (26 metre) dive into just 10 feet (3 metres) of water.

The Kennedy monument at Runnymede.

10
Surrey people

Its location, close to London, yet quietly rural, has long attracted people to Surrey. For many, Surrey has been no more than a temporary home, but for a few it has become more permanent. In particular, Surrey has long had an association with writers.

Sir James Matthew Barrie (1860-1937) was born in Scotland but cultivated some success in selling articles to London papers during his time with the *Nottingham Journal.* This encouraged him to move south and from 1900 to 1909 he lived at Lobsworth Manor, near Black Lake, Tilford. It was during this time that he wrote *Peter Pan.*

Lewis Carroll (1832-98) often stayed with his sisters at The Chestnuts, Castle Street, Guildford, where he died. Born Charles Lutwidge Dodgson, he was a mathematician, but a very shy man. He spoke with a stammer but got on well with children. His character Alice was based on a child he befriended in Oxford, but it has been suggested that his inspiration for the Cheshire Cat in *Alice in Wonderland* came from a carving in Cranleigh parish church. Sculptures in Guildford recall his connections with the town and objects and letters associated with the author are housed in the museum.

One of Farnham's best-known sons is **William Cobbett** (1763-1835), who was born at the inn in Bridge Square now known as the William Cobbett. Famed for his *Rural Rides*, which give fascinating glimpses of country life in the 1820s, he was also a politician and was the founder of Hansard, the record of Parliamentary debate. He died at his farm in Normandy and is buried at Farnham.

George Sturt lived in The Borough district of Farnham. His books describe life in and around Farnham during the second half of the nineteenth century and include *Change in the Village, The Wheelwright's Shop* and *A Small Boy in the Sixties.*

The attractive countryside around Waverley Abbey was the temporary home of Edinburgh-born **Sir Arthur Conan Doyle** (1859-1930). Later he moved to Hindhead, where his house, Undershaw, is now an hotel. His *White Company* novels are set in the area and Sir Nigel's ancient house of Loring is based upon Tilford House.

William Cobbett's tomb by the door of Farnham church.

The area around Waverley Abbey was home to other writers too. In the seventeenth century **Sir William Temple** (1628-99), moved first to Sheen, then later to Moor Park, near Farnham, after he retired as a diplomat. Here he produced several volumes of essays.

His secretary was **Jonathan Swift** (1667-1745). Born in Ireland, the son of a Yorkshire vicar, he spent four years at Moor Park, between 1690 and 1694. He had been preparing for his MA but had only a bachelor's degree when he came to Farnham. He probably hoped that his connection with Sir William would be beneficial, but although Temple did recommend him for various posts, nothing came of them. It was at Farnham that Swift began to write, and he later achieved renown as a poet and satirist, although his best-known works, including *Gulliver's Travels* (1714), were published after Temple's death and his departure from Moor Park.

The poet **Alfred, Lord Tennyson** (1809-92) also moved houses regularly during his life but settled in Haslemere in 1868, where he lived at Aldworth on Blackdown until his death. There is a memorial window to him in Haslemere parish church.

The prolific novelist and poet **George Meredith** (1828-1909) is probably best-known for his novel *Diana of the Crossways*, said to have been set at Crossways Farm, Abinger Hammer. He boarded at Weybridge after his marriage to Thomas Peacock's daughter and later settled at Lower Halliford. She deserted him in 1858, after which he moved to a house near Esher. In 1864, when he married Marie Vulliamy, he moved to Flint Cottage at the foot of Box Hill's Zig Zag Road. His second wife died in 1889, but Meredith remained at Flint Cottage until his own death, writing in a study he had built at the top of the garden. A memorial service was held at Westminster Abbey on the day of his funeral but he is buried in Dorking Cemetery.

Matthew Arnold (1822-88), son of Thomas Arnold, headmaster of Rugby School, was born at Laleham. In 1843 he won the Newdigate Prize for poetry and became a fellow of Oriel College in 1845. He was a strong supporter of educational reform, working tirelessly to improve secondary education

Matthew Arnold's grave at Laleham is covered with daffodils in the spring.

in England. However, he is best-known as a writer, poet and critic. From 1873 he lived at Painshill Cottage, Cobham, and although he died in Liverpool he is buried at Laleham.

George Eliot (1819-80) moved to Holly Lodge, Wimbledon, during a particularly difficult period of her life. She shared the house with the critic George Henry Lewes and whilst there wrote *The Mill on the Floss*.

The writer **John Evelyn** (1620-1706) is best-known for his *Diary*. However, he also wrote several other works including *Sylva*, a book on practical arboriculture. A founder member of the Royal Society, he was born at the family seat, Wotton House, where he designed and laid out the gardens. He is buried at St John's church, Wotton.

A very different type of writer was **Aldous Leonard Huxley** (1894-1963), author of

Brave New World. He was born in Peperharow Road, Godalming, and his father was a master at Charterhouse School. Although he settled in California from the late 1930s he is buried at Compton Cemetery.

One of Surrey's most famous inhabitants is **Gertrude Jekyll** (1843-1932), the well-known garden designer. Miss Jekyll was born in Godalming, spent her childhood in Bramley and later lived at Busbridge. Her country cottage gardens complemented much of the work of **Sir Edwin Landseer Lutyens** (1869-1944), one of Britain's greatest architects. He spent many of his early years in Thursley and dozens of his cottages can still be seen in west Surrey. Among his other architectural projects are included Hampstead Garden Suburb, New Delhi and the British pavilion at the Paris exhibition. Jekyll's association with Lutyens continued, even after her death. She is buried at Busbridge in a tomb designed by the architect.

Lutyens's work extended far beyond Surrey, as did that of **James Edward Oglethorpe** (1696-1785). He lived at Westbrook House in Godalming and was the founder of the American state of Georgia.

Another statesman, **Richard Bedford Bennet** (1870-1947), travelled the other way. He was Prime Minister of Canada from 1930 to 1935. Born in New Brunswick, he led a full political career in Canada, retiring to England in 1938 following an election defeat. He was made a Viscount in 1941 and is buried in Mickleham churchyard.

The conductor and impresario **Sir Thomas Beecham** (1879-1961) is buried at Brookwood Cemetery near Woking. He founded the London Philharmonic Orchestra in 1931 and was much connected with the London music scene.

Beecham did much to promote the work of the composer **Frederick Delius** (1862-1934), who is buried in St Peter's churchyard, Limpsfield. Delius was born of German parents, who discouraged him from following a musical career. Although he lived the last fifty years of his life in France and was temporarily buried in the churchyard at Grez-sur-Loing, his body was brought to Limpsfield, where Sir Thomas Beecham read the funeral oration.

Still well remembered in Surrey is the Gloucestershire-born composer **Ralph Vaughan Williams** (1872-1958). Part of his education was gained at Charterhouse School and he lived for many years on the slopes of Leith Hill. He did much to promote music through the annual Leith Hill Music Festival, which continues today.

Those to whom odd machines appeal will have heard of **William Heath Robinson** (1872-1944). This illustrator and cartoonist, well-known for his humorous pictures of strange contraptions, lived in Cranleigh for twenty years.

The more serious side of science is represented by **John Flamsteed** (1646-1719), who took a great interest in astronomy from his youngest days. The son of a maltster from Derby, he left school early because of ill health. Even so, by the age of sixteen he had observed a partial eclipse of the sun and attempted to make astronomical instruments. At Cambridge he became known to Isaac Newton and after gaining his MA was appointed 'astronomical observator' by Charles II at the age of twenty-nine. He later quarrelled with Newton over their results and failed to see the complete publication of his major astronomical work before his death. He was ordained and in 1684 obtained the living of Burstow church, where he is buried.

One of the greatest revolutions in the biological sciences was the development of the theory of evolution. Although often credited to **Charles Darwin** (1809-82), it was the work of both him and **Alfred Russel Wallace** (1823-1913). Wallace lived in Croydon for one year and Darwin stayed several times in the countryside around Dorking, Abinger and Leith Hill.

Another man who had a profound effect on everyday life was **Professor John Tyndall** (1820-93), who lived at Hindhead. He began life as an Irish railway engineer but continually strove to improve himself, eventually winning the patronage of Michael Faraday. He had an interest in anything to do with light, sound or heat and discovered the connection between decay and airborne germs.

Frederick George Creed (1871-1957), the inventor of the teleprinter, was born in Glasgow but lived for over fifty years in Croydon. He was to see his invention widely adapted by newspaper offices throughout Britain.

Gardeners everywhere recognise the name of John Innes potting compost. It is named after **John Innes** (1829-1904), who founded the John Innes Horticultural Institute during his thirty-year residence at Merton Park.

Sir Walter Raleigh (c.1552-1618) is probably best-known as the person who introduced tobacco and potatoes to England. An explorer and writer, he found favour with Queen Elizabeth I, but not with James I, who sent him to the Tower for many years. While there he wrote his *History of the World.* After his release he led a disastrous expedition to the Orinoco. When he returned to Britain he was executed and his decapitated body was buried in St Margaret's Church, Westminster. His wife, however, apparently had his head embalmed and carried it around with her until she died. It is now buried at West Horsley.

The Effingham area contains plenty of references to **Charles, Baron Howard of Effingham** (1536-1624). He was Lord High Admiral at the time of the Spanish Armada and also a Commissioner at the trials of Mary, Queen of Scots, and the Gunpowder Plot conspirators.

Few people would recognise the name of Welshman John Rowlands (1841-1904), nor connect him with a granite monument in Pirbright to Bula Matari. However, Rowlands went to sea when young, eventually arriving in New Orleans, where he was adopted by a cotton broker, whose name, **Henry Morton Stanley**, Rowlands took as his own. Later, while working for the *New York Times,* he was sent by the proprietor, Gordon Bennett, to find Dr David Livingstone, who was missing in the African interior. On his return to Britain he was knighted, elected a Member of Parliament and settled at Pirbright, where he is buried. The monument records the African version of his name.

It is perhaps fitting to end with another explorer, **Lawrence Oates** (1880-1912). Between the ages of five and eleven he lived in Roehampton. Later he developed a taste for travel and went on to become an Antarctic explorer, joining Scott's expedition which reached the South Pole in 1912. On the return journey he was suffering so badly from frostbite that he was slowing down the progress of the rest of the team. He left his tent during a blizzard saying: 'I am just going outside and may be some time.' He was never seen again.

11

Legends, traditions and festivals

In comparison with other parts of Britain, there are few traditional customs and events in Surrey. There are, however, a large number of modern events and festivals.

Stories, legends and ghosts are more commonplace and Surrey has been described as the most haunted county in Britain. Apart from the more usual type of ghostly sightings, Surrey is said to have several phantom coaches and even, in west Surrey, a phantom house. In Mollison Drive on the Roundshaw Estate at Croydon a ghost riding a motorcycle has been seen. He is believed to be an airman who died while the site was Croydon Airport.

The last witch to be hanged in Surrey lived in Dorking until 1665. Yet, in the eighteenth century, a witch known as Mother Ludlam is supposed to have inhabited a cave near Waverley Abbey. A large copper cauldron, now in Frensham church, is reputed to have belonged to her. Another story states that the Devil can be raised by running around Frensham church seven times after seven o'clock in the evening.

South of Guildford stand two hilltop chapels, St Martha's and St Catherine's, on opposite sides of the valley. These are said to have been built by two giantesses, who had only had one hammer between them. They threw it back and forth across the valley, which supposedly explains why Guildfordians have flat heads.

Legends are more frequent in western Surrey than the east. A soldier condemned for desertion is said to have offered to kill a dragon which used to prowl West Clandon, in return for a reprieve. The story has been commemorated by cutting an image of a dragon into the chalk embankment of the A246.

In more recent times another mysterious beast has reportedly been seen around the county. Reports of the Surrey puma, extremely frequent in the early 1970s, are now dying out.

Tunnels linking historic buildings are frequently mentioned in literature about the county. Undoubtedly some passages do exist, many of which have collapsed so that their full extent cannot be explored. Others, such as the so-called caves in Dorking, were dug out by eccentric people and later used as wine cellars. In 1984 some tunnels were found in Leatherhead and many people claimed they were once the hiding place of the notorious Judge Jeffreys. Their pointed bottoms would have made standing up in them extremely difficult.

Many stories, such as those which claim King John frightened a local girl into drowning at the Silent Pool, have origins in novels.

Very few calendar customs existed in Surrey. Several that did related to 'husband divining' – various methods that a girl could use to identify her future husband, on Valentine's Eve.

A strange custom that used to take place if someone disapproved of his neighbour's behaviour was known as rough music. The aggrieved person gathered together a group of friends and some old cans, and they then made as much noise as possible outside the door of the offending neighbour around three o'clock in the morning.

Bringing in the May is one of the customs recently revived by Matthew Alexander, curator of Guildford Museum. The custom involves morris dancing on certain hilltops at daybreak on May Day.

Hallowe'en has been celebrated in the south of England only since the late nineteenth century. This evening of ghosts and witches is usually a good excuse for fancy dress parties.

Since the eighteenth century bonfires and fireworks have been used to celebrate Guy Fawkes Night. 5th November is now relatively calm, although some of the Surrey bonfires are claimed to be the largest in Britain, especially that at Brockham, which attracts people from all over the

Epsom racecourse is the annual venue for the Derby.

area. Until 1863, however, 5th November used to be feared for the violent riots that took place in towns such as Guildford.

Many towns in the county have regular shows and carnivals, and most villages hold summer fetes and flower shows. One of the largest agricultural shows in Britain is the Surrey County Show, held in Stoke Park, Guildford, at the end of May.

There is a long artistic tradition in Surrey, especially in the field of music. Ralph Vaughan Williams lived near Dorking and performed at the first Leith Hill Music Festival. An offshoot of this has been the annual performance of Handel's *Messiah* in St Martin's church, Dorking.

In the field of sport, the Derby at Epsom is the most famous event to take place in Surrey. Yet there are many other sporting contests, including Sunbury Regatta and Cranleigh Lawn Tennis Championships.

March/April
Leith Hill Music Festival, Dorking Halls.

May
Surrey County Show, Stoke Park, Guildford.

Summer
Sheepdog trials, throughout the Mole valley area.

June
The Derby, Epsom.
Abinger Medieval Fair.
Guildford Festival: a range of events including exhibitions, shows, films and canoe racing.
National Rifle Association Championships, Bisley.

July/August
Thorndike Film Festival, Leatherhead (eight weeks).

August
Sunbury Regatta.
Cranleigh Agricultural Show.
Farnham Town Show.
Cranleigh Lawn Tennis Championships.

September
Chertsey Show.
Guildford Town Show.
Thursley Exhibition.

October
Surrey Antiques Fair, Civic Hall, Guildford.
World Match Play Golf Championships, Wentworth.

November
Bonfires, at Brockham and elsewhere.
Handel's *Messiah*, St Martin's church, Dorking.

12
Tourist information centres

Camberley: Haywood House, 1 Portesbery Road, Camberley GU15 7DR. Telephone: 01276 692437.

Croydon: Croydon Clocktower, Katharine Street, Croydon CR9 1ET. Telephone: 0181-253 1009.

Farnham: Vernon House, 28 West Street, Farnham GU9 7DR. Telephone: 01252 715109.

Guildford: 14 Tunsgate, Guildford GU1 3QT. Telephone: 01483 444007.

Richmond: Old Town Hall, Whittaker Avenue, Richmond TW9 1TP. Telephone: 0181-940 9125.

The Maori house in the grounds of Clandon Park.

13
Further reading

Brandon, P. *A History of Surrey.* Phillimore, 1977.

Chapman, G., and Young, R. *Box Hill.* Serendip, 1979.

Cherry, B., and Pevsner, N. *The Buildings of England: London 2: South.* Penguin, 1983.

Drewett, J. *The Nature of Surrey.* Barracuda, 1987.

Drewett, P.; Rudling, D.; and Gardiner, M. *The South East to AD 1000.* Longman, 1988.

Fletcher Jones, P. *Richmond Park.* Phillimore, 1972.

Fortescue, S.E.D. *People and Places: Great and Little Bookham.* Fortescue, 1978.

Howkins, C. *Hidden Surrey.* Countryside Books, 1987.

Jackson, A.A. (editor). *Ashtead, A Village Transformed.* Leatherhead and District Local History Society, 1977.

Lousley, J.E. *Flora of Surrey.* David & Charles, 1976.

Mackworth-Praed, H. *Conservation Pieces.* Packard, 1991.

Nairn, I., and Pevsner, N. *The Buildings of England: Surrey.* Penguin, 1971.

Parr, D. (editor). *Birds in Surrey.* Batsford, 1972.

Weinreb, B., and Hibbert, C. (editors). *The London Encyclopaedia.* Dictionary of London Ltd, 1983.

Wooldridge, S.W., and Goldring, F. *The Weald.* Collins, 1953.

Index

Page numbers in italic refer to illustrations.